The Tools of Leadership

Frederic W. Skoglund

Foreword by Lawrence W. Lezotte

ROWMAN & LITTLEFIELD EDUCATION

A division of
ROWMAN & LITTLEFIELD PUBLISHERS, INC.
Lanham • Boulder • New York • Toronto • Plymouth, UK

Published by Rowman & Littlefield Education
A division of Rowman & Littlefield
4501 Forbes Boulevard, Suite 200, Lanham, Maryland 20706
www.rowman.com

10 Thornbury Road, Plymouth PL6 7PP, United Kingdom

Copyright © 2013 by Frederic W. Skoglund

All rights reserved. No part of this book may be reproduced in any form or by any electronic or mechanical means, including information storage and retrieval systems, without written permission from the publisher, except by a reviewer who may quote passages in a review.

British Library Cataloguing in Publication Information Available

Library of Congress Cataloging-in-Publication Data

Skoglund, Frederic, 1945–
  The tools of leadership / Frederic W. Skoglund ; Foreword by Lawrence W. Lezotte.
    pages cm
  Includes bibliographical references.
    ISBN 978-1-4758-0523-9 (cloth)— ISBN 978-1-4758-0524-6 (pbk.)— ISBN 978-1-4758-0525-3 (electronic)
    1. Educational leadership. 2. School management and organization. I. Title.
  LB2806.S54 2013
  371.2—dc23   2013022305

For Kathy,
the love of my life.

Thank you for always making things better.

Contents

Foreword by Dr. Lawrence W. Lezotte		vii
Preface by Judy Ness		ix
Introduction		xi
1	Is Your School Effective? Dr. Lawrence Lezotte, "Effective Schools: Past, Present, and Future"	1
2	Meeting Our Basic Needs: Dr. William Glasser, *Control Theory*	13
3	Don't Forget Your Change! Dr. Gene Hall, *Implementing Change: Patterns, Principles, and Potholes*	21
4	Get With It! Dr. Frederick Herzberg, *The Motivation to Work*	33
5	The System Did It! Dr. Peter Senge, *The Fifth Discipline: The Art & Practice of the Learning Organization* and *Schools That Learn*	45
6	The Mind Map	71
7	The Perfect Storm	81
References		85
Suggested Readings		87
About the Author		89

Foreword

More than thirty years ago, my now-deceased colleague, Ron Edmonds, made a profound and timeless statement about the importance of leadership in creating and maintaining an effective school. He stated that he had found effective principals leading schools that were not *yet* effective. Thus effective leadership was a *necessary* but not sufficient condition for ensuring school effectiveness. He went on to add that he had never found an effective school that did not have an effective leader as principal. One would have hoped that after three decades of studies we could say with pride and certainty that our eighty-thousand-plus public schools are currently being led by effective principals. Unfortunately, this is simply not the case. We've made progress but no one would deny that we still have a long way to go. Why is this so?

A partial answer to the problem can be found in the fact that we can't seem to agree on what is meant by effective leadership. Effective leadership, like beauty, is said to be in the eye of the beholder. Some look only at organizational results or outcomes and, if they agree with them, declare that they were achieved because of effective leadership, with no consideration to the methods used by the leader. Sometimes the title of effective leadership is awarded based on the methods used by the leader. They essentially ignore the actual results achieved (i.e., professional learning communities). Sometimes an individual is celebrated as an effective leader because of the leader's personality—he or she is well liked, and the staff has high morale. The different effective leadership perspectives beg the question, "Which perspective is correct?"

In every decade, literally millions of words on the topic of leadership are written or spoken. If one were to pick the most popular leadership publications in any decade and analyze them, a relatively short list of descriptive concepts would surface as those most frequently and directly associated with effective leadership. Among these, one would find the following: "visionary," "purpose," "mission driven," "monitoring," "metrics," "cheerleader," "coach," "caring," "communicator," "trustworthy," "change agent," "competent," "enthusiastic," "inspiring," and "motivator."

In today's schools, *results* and the use of *selected concepts* have to be given the highest priority because they have been proven to work. Failure of school leaders to focus on the high-priority concepts can be catastrophic for the most needy children that schools are expected to educate.

If effective school leaders don't already naturally exist, can we teach the most important of these concepts to aspiring candidates? *The Tools of Leadership* manuscript provides us with proof that we can.

Fortunately, as you'll read shortly, Skoglund's framework emphasizes a shorter list of high-priority concepts. The framework set forth in *Tools of Leadership* focuses heavily on being mission driven, monitoring, motivation, communication, and change. The author has done an excellent job of linking each of these priority concepts to the research and writings of at least one of the most celebrated scholars who have written on the topic of effective leadership. It is said that researchers and change advocates owe it to the reader to identify and acknowledge those who have gone before and upon whose shoulders he stands. Skoglund has done so with great clarity.

In *The Tools of Leadership*, powerful writings by outstanding research scholars have been woven together into a framework for action. The framework has been tested and found to be valid in making schools more effective for more students. The author has woven a new tapestry of possibilities for advancing the effective school leadership agenda and with it the school's mission of learning for all. We must not wait another three decades before we make good on the promise of an effective leader in every school.

Lawrence W. Lezotte

Preface

Welcome. My name is Judy Ness and two years ago I had the privilege to coauthor *Student Success: How to Make It Happen* with Dr. Frederic W. Skoglund, the author of the book you are about to read.

There are a few things that I would encourage you to do as you read *The Tools of Leadership*.

- Keep a journal handy and jot down any "ahas," insights, questions, and inspirations that occur to you. I assure you that there will be many.
- Read the books written by the amazing authors identified in Fred's "toolbox." If you do not have a copy, check the library or an online distributor.
- If at all possible, read this book with colleagues from your profession and/or other professions. It provides a wide range of applications that will help leaders improve their effectiveness.

Because they are intended to be companion books, I encourage you to read *Student Success: How to Make It Happen* first and then follow up with *The Tools of Leadership*. With this two-part collection of knowledge, you will be able to lead an even more effective implementation of the Continuous Improvement System that was presented in *Student Success*.

The book is not long but it is full of a mix of the "tried and true" and the "innovative and new." For too long, we have been discarding important previously gained wisdom for the newest ideas. Both have value and should be used together.

In this book, Fred clearly shows you how to accomplish this. He helps you form a systematic approach that allows you to benefit from the wisdom of Gene Hall, Frederick Herzberg, William Glasser, Larry Lezotte, and Peter Senge. He also shows you how to use their proven wisdom individually and collectively as you seek to lead your organization to higher performance levels.

Writing a book with Fred was an honor and a privilege. I thought that I was a good synthesis thinker who could see the obvious and not so obvious connections and interactions of people and processes in a system. Next to Fred, I am lucky to be rated average. He can see connections that most of us do not see. Most importantly, in these two books, he helps educational leaders implement a system to improve teacher performance, enhance student achievement, and make the connections necessary to effectively use the tools of leadership in any personal or professional setting.

I am confident that those whom you lead will enjoy having a systems-thinking leader. I wish you all the success I know is possible by taking to heart what Fred has to share. The rewards and returns are enormous!

Judy Ness

Introduction

PLACE YOUR BETS!

There is an old adage that has frequently been heard at racetracks and in corporate boardrooms alike. It states, "Bet on the jockey and not on the horse." This is such an intriguing and provocative statement that in the late 1990s, research was conducted to assess its veracity.

Photo I.1

In one study, the Fast Company Consultant Debunking Unit (Chadderdon 1999) followed two of the top jockeys at Churchill Downs and the 347 horses they rode during the season. In a second study, the financial backing decisions of venture capitalists were observed as they considered new products that entrepreneurs were attempting to bring to market. Here are the conclusions drawn from these studies:

1. If you are at the racetrack, bet on the horse.
2. If you are in the boardroom, bet on the jockey.

At the track, a reasonably competent jockey is needed but the quality of the horse is the deciding factor in the race. In the business world, a great idea or product may never see the light of day except for the competence, commitment, and passion of even a single person.

In *Student Success: How to Make It Happen*, my colleague, Judy Ness, and I gave you the horse. We described how to implement and facilitate the Continuous Improvement System (see page xvii for a review of the CIS). The CIS has proven itself to be a thoroughbred in the race toward school improvement. It is a very effective system; however, the bottom line is that it must be implemented with fidelity and operated by dedicated and competent people because no system, no matter how good it is, can overcome indifference and/or incompetent performance by the people who are using it. The leadership demonstrated by the principal is essential to the success of the CIS. I want to stress again a point that we made in *Student Success*: typically, successful organizations have a competent and effective leader at the top of the organization. Successful organizations also have effective leaders at every level within the organization. The CIS is designed to be a system that the principal facilitates while delegating leadership responsibility to individuals across the entire faculty.

Therefore, it is critical that principals and other educational leaders develop the skills they need to bring out the best in the people with whom they work. This is not a simple task. In fact, it is one of the most complicated and challenging tasks that any leader will face. This book will provide leaders with a set of tools that will help them become the best jockeys they can be.

During my career, I have assembled a "toolbox" of skills. I have studied the work of five men for many years and have very carefully and purposefully chosen to include them in my toolbox. Each of these men has created an impressive body of work and made significant contributions to his field.

Employed individually, the "tools" they have created will help any leader to become more effective. However, when one grasps how their

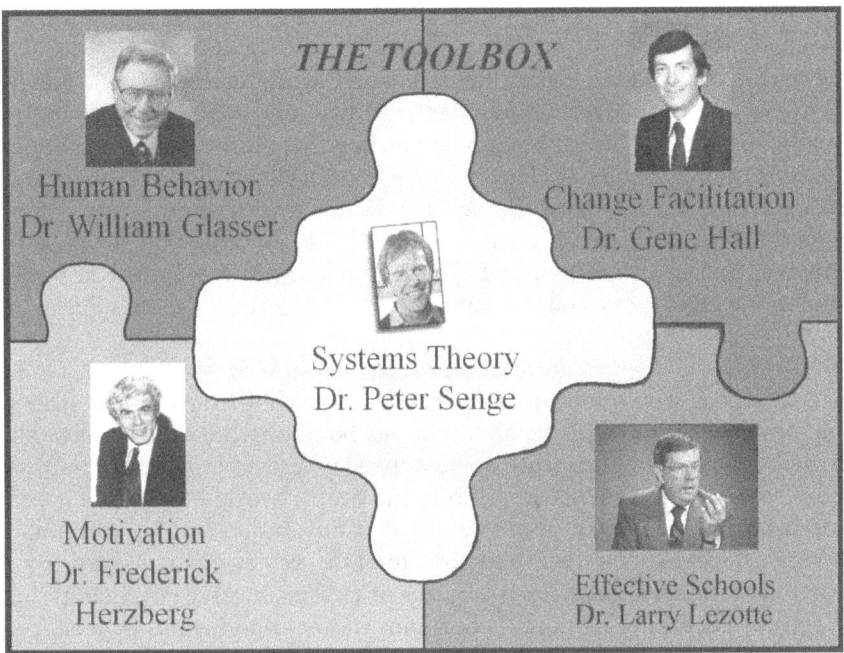

Photo I.2. Printed by permission of Dr. William Glasser, Dr. Gene Hall, Dr. Lawrence Lezotte, and Dr. Peter Senge.

individual works interact and come together as pieces of a wonderful puzzle, the effectiveness of that person will increase exponentially. Solving this puzzle brings the realization that these tools are applicable in *any* interpersonal or organizational setting. These tools are equally valuable to a school principal, an entrepreneur running a small business, the CEO of a Fortune 500 company, or an adult child faced with the terrible task of taking the car keys from an elderly parent.

Dr. Gene Hall is currently a professor in the School of Environmental and Public Affairs at the University of Nevada, Las Vegas. During his time at the University of Texas, he served as the director of the Research and Development Center for Teacher Education. The research he conducted there produced the Concerns-Based Adoption Model (CBAM). This work identified a series of concerns that people experience when they face change. Dr. Hall determined that people will seldom embrace a change until their concerns are alleviated, and thus he identified appropriate interventions. He is highly respected in the educational community for his work in facilitating change in organizations. The CBAM is used by change agents worldwide.

Dr. Frederick Herzberg (1923–2000) was a lecturer and professor of management in the College of Business at the University of Utah. He was recognized as one of the most influential people working in the field of business management. His research identified two sets of factors found in the workplace. One set produced job satisfaction and thus encouraged people to perform at high levels. The other set produced job dissatisfaction and led to lower levels of performance. He created a vertical job loading process that was designed to create a motivational environment for people. His publication, *One More Time: How Do You Motivate Employees?*, remains one of the most requested documents from the *Harvard Business Review*.

Dr. William Glasser is an internationally recognized psychiatrist. He is the creator of a revolutionary approach to psychotherapy called reality therapy. He set forth his technique in his book titled *Reality Therapy*. He is the founder of the Institute for Reality Therapy, an institution that has now served over seventy-five thousand people worldwide. His following book, *Choice Theory*, greatly expanded our understanding of human behavior. He has been honored with the Life Achievement Award from the International Center for the Study of Psychiatry and Psychology for his groundbreaking work and enormous influence in field of psychiatry.

Dr. Larry Lezotte is professor emeritus at Michigan State University. During his tenure at MSU, he served as the chair of the Department of Educational Administration and associate director of the Center for School Improvement. He was one of the original researchers who identified the Correlates of Effective Schools and is known as the preeminent spokesperson for effective schools research and implementation. He has been awarded the Brock International Prize in Education for his contributions to the science of education.

Dr. Peter Senge is the senior lecturer in Leadership and Sustainability at the Massachusetts Institute of Technology's Sloan School of Management. He set forth incredibly insightful concepts in his best-selling book, *The Fifth Discipline*. He is the founder of the Society for Organizational Learning. The esteem in which he is held was demonstrated when the *Journal of Business Strategy* named him one of the twenty-four people who have had the greatest influence on business strategy during the past one hundred years.

Put yourself in the position of a principal charged with the task of raising the level of student achievement in a school. What general plan would you follow to accomplish the task?

It seems logical that the first step would be to learn about the characteristics of schools that are producing high levels of student achievement. The research on effective schools done by Dr. Lezotte and his colleagues clearly describes seven conditions (correlates) that are present in high-performing schools and absent in low-performing schools. These should be a guide to a successful plan to elevate the level of student achievement.

Dr. Senge's work on systems teaches us that a school (or any organization) is more than a group of individual components. The Effective Schools Correlates are not mutually exclusive. They are interactive components of a complicated system that is a school. Significant improvement will not be accomplished by focusing on only one correlate. Tinkering with only one component of a system will simply cause the other components to be out of balance.

When you have a clear picture of what you want the school to look like and how you want it to function, your focus must shift to the people who will be asked to make the changes and produce the new and more effective school. The fact that most people typically resist change reflects a natural human behavior. Change causes people to be concerned about such things as how the change will impact them personally and what new demands will be made upon their time. Dr. Hall's Concerns-Based Adoption Model (CBAM) provides ways to identify the concerns that people are experiencing and interventions that will alleviate the concerns and allow the people to move forward in the acceptance of a change.

This is critical because the people in an organization *must* change before the organization *can* change.

In order for any leader to effectively work with his or her colleagues, the leader must understand human behavior and why we act as we do. Dr. Glasser's work provides solid insight into this fascinating field.

Once the change process has begun, leaders must find ways to create an environment in which people will choose to consistently put forth their best effort. Dr. Herzberg's work on motivation in the workplace is an invaluable guide to creating such an environment.

This book will help school (or any organizational) leaders to understand how the pieces of the puzzle form a system that can be used to implement and facilitate a plan to elevate any person's performance.

Chapters 1–5 in the book will consist of five sections:

1. The first section will describe the work of one of the men pictured in the toolbox. The information presented is a concise discussion of what I gleaned from reading the publication identified next to the author's name. The information I will share with you is accurate, and

you will be able to make effective but basic use of it. Albert Einstein wisely stated, "A little knowledge is a dangerous thing." Obviously, the more knowledge you have before you begin to use the tool, the more successful your initial attempts will be and the better you will be prepared to deal with the surprises that are inevitable. For this reason, I urge you to read the entire publication as well as other related works by the author.
2. In the second section, I will tell you a story about a single fictional character. Each of the situations and conversations described are true although they actually occurred with three different individuals. The persona of the fictional character of Sarge is based on an actual person. Weaving these individual situations and conversations into one story is intended to help you understand how the tools were used individually and in conjunction with others to address difficult situations in both the personal and professional domains.
3. The third section will give an explanation of which tool(s) I chose to use in that situation and why.
4. The fourth section will be a chapter summary that will very briefly review the key points of the chapter.
5. The final section is a workbook section where you will be asked to accomplish a task.

If you have not read *Student Success: How to Make It Happen*, the following description and discussion of the components will give you a basic understanding of the Continuous Improvement System.

The CIS was created after a review of the many school improvement programs that have emerged during the past several years. The exhaustive efforts to improve schools during that time appear to have produced little significant and sustainable results. I am convinced that one of the primary reasons for these results is that the programs that were implemented were very narrow in focus. They would focus on curriculum with no attention being given to instruction. They would focus on creating valid formative assessments with no attention being given to how to make immediate and effective use of the data. These school improvement programs simply viewed the school as a collection of parts and not as a complex whole. The Continuous Improvement System takes a very different approach. The systematic approach of the CIS is intended to bring together all aspects of the teaching and learning process.

One of the first issues that was considered in creating the CIS was replacing the teacher isolation that is typical in most US schools with collaboration. In our schools, teachers spend the vast majority of their time working alone and principals are frequently asked to carry the mantle of leadership alone. This is the antithesis of how schools function in the countries that consistently rank above the United States in international academic comparisons.

The CIS broadens the role of leadership to include educators at all levels of the school. A leadership team is formed and facilitated by the principal. The work of the leadership team is driven by the analysis of real-time formative assessment data. The data collected depicts the performance of individual students, each classroom, and each grade level or subject. The data is made visible to all who work in or visit the school. This practice is a powerful force that drives students and teachers alike to consistently put forth their best efforts.

Figure I.1 and the explanations of the individual components that appear on the following pages will give you an overview of the CIS.

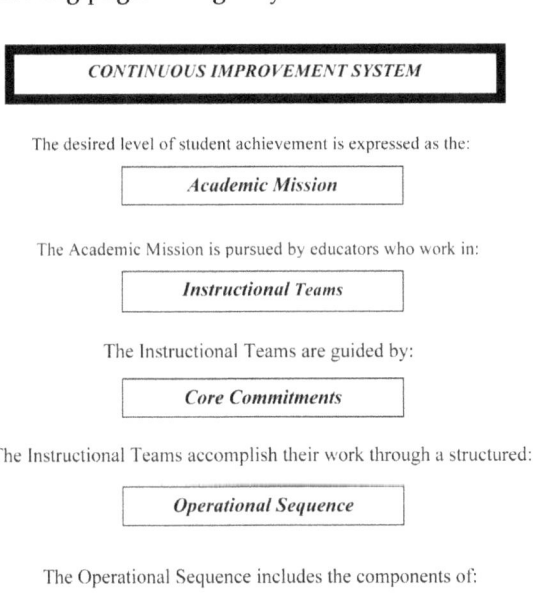

Figure I.1

ACADEMIC MISSION

Think of this in the military sense. If a team of Navy SEALs is sent on a mission, they know exactly what they are to accomplish and how success will be determined.

The faculty identifies the level of expected student achievement and accepts the responsibility to achieve it. The mission must be set at a level high enough to stretch both the faculty and students. It must, however, be set at a reasonable and attainable level. It sets a bar that is raised when the level of achievement is consistently achieved.

This is a critical process and you must anticipate that it will take time, open and honest dialogue, patience, and some amount of teeth gnashing as teachers proclaim, "But my class is different!" The level of the academic mission is intended for all classrooms. The only possible exception(s) to be considered might be an honors class or a special education situation.

EXAMPLE: We, the faculty of _____ School, ensure that X percent of our students will achieve a minimum of Y percent correct answers on all formative assessments.

The academic mission is displayed in every classroom, the data room, the school lobby, and in other prominent locations throughout the school.

INSTRUCTIONAL TEAMS

Instructional teams are groups of teachers who teach the same grade level or the same subject matter. The CIS requires teachers to work in these collaborative teams.

CORE COMMITMENTS

These statements are written by the faculty. They identify specific and observable behaviors that educators commit to exhibit as they work to accomplish the academic mission.

EXAMPLE: We, the faculty of _____ School, commit to work in collaborative instructional teams in order to achieve our academic mission.

This document is displayed in every classroom, the data room, the school lobby, and in other prominent locations throughout the school.

Introduction

OPERATIONAL SEQUENCE

The activities included in these components are critical to the successful implementation and operation of the CIS.

- The CIS spreads the responsibility for effective leadership over administrators and faculty members. No individual working alone can do all that must be done.
- The curriculum is set by state and national standards and instruction is based on research-proven instructional strategies and materials.
- Teachers use common formative assessments that mirror the end-of-year high-stakes test in content, language, format, and rigor.
- Data is collected at three levels: (1) on individual students, (2) from individual classrooms, and (3) across a grade level or subject matter. The timely and accurate depiction of this data is used to drive instruction.
- Administrators evaluate teacher performance in both instructional and noninstructional activities. This process is used in job status decisions.

TOOLS

- The instructional teams, the leadership team, and the faculty meet on a regular basis and follow agendas that include specific standing items.
- The standing agenda items address upcoming curriculum, common assessments, achievement data, instructional strategies, and plans for assisting students who are not performing at the level identified in the academic mission.

Instructional Calendar		4th Grade Math		September
Monday	Tuesday	Wednesday	Thursday	Friday
S2-C4-PO6 Common Denominator	⟶	S3-C2-PO 7 Add common fractions	⟶	Formative Assessment

Figure I.2

- Instructional teams collaborate to create a flexible schedule for curriculum and assessments. The calendars are focused on the performance objectives identified in the state standards. The only reference to a textbook is to identify the location of the objective in the text. This document is displayed in classrooms and the data room.
- Instructional teams collaborate to create formative assessments that are used by all teachers in a grade level or subject. The items are selected from examples in the core standards, previous state tests, and other question banks that are valid and reliable. The assessments are constructed in a way that makes it easy for teachers to identify specific objectives that students are having difficulty in mastering.

S3 – C2 –PO7			
1.	Add 3/5 and 1/4	2.	Find the sum of 7/8 and 1/6
3.	Add 5/8 and 2/9	4.	Find the sum of 1/2 and 1/6

Figure I.3

- Data from the common formative assessments is depicted on three charts that track individual student performance, the performance of all students in a given classroom, and the performance of all students in a grade level or subject.
- Individual students monitor their own performance on a chart that contains a bold line set at the level of correct responses identified in the academic mission. This chart significantly impacts the motivation to learn and serves as a powerful tool during parent conferences.
- The classroom data charts contain a bold line set at the percent of students in the class who are expected to meet or exceed the level identified in the academic mission. This is maintained by each teacher and posted in the classroom next to the instructional calendar. These are also posted in the data room. The combination of the calendar and the data chart allows the principal to enter the classroom and, within seconds, determine what has been taught and how well students in that room mastered the performance objectives. These charts are the primary tool used by teachers during their instructional team meetings.
- The grade-level / subject data charts contain a bold line set at the percent of students across the entire grade level / subject who are expected to meet or exceed the level identified in the academic mission. The charts are posted in the data room where the leadership team meets. They create a clear picture of student achievement across the school. These charts are the primary tool used by the leadership team during their meetings.

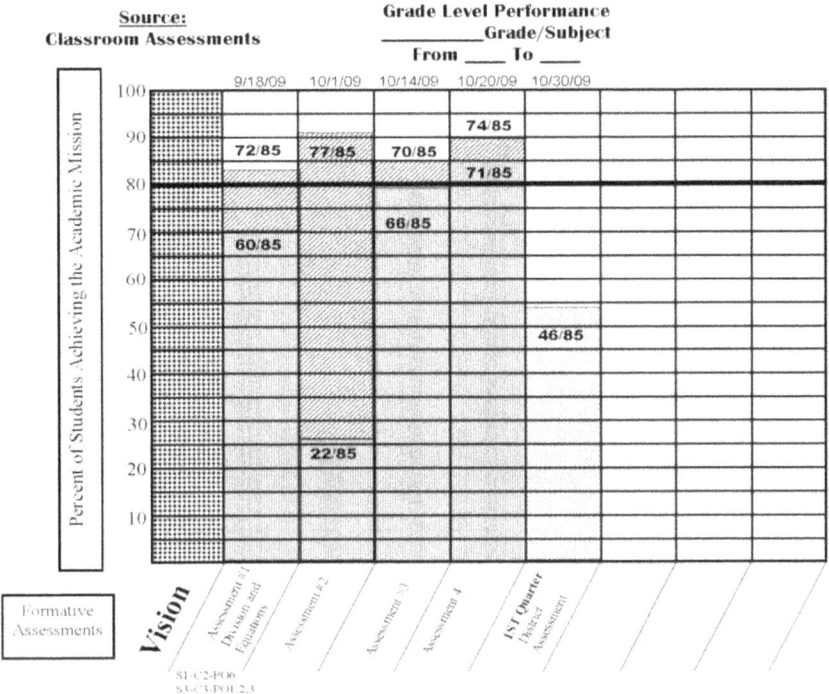

Figure I.4

There is an ongoing dialogue among administrators, teachers, and curriculum/instruction specialists. The primary focus is proven strategies and materials. Teachers are never evaluated based on student achievement data alone; however, this data may alert an administrator to ineffective instruction and cause the administrator to observe a specific classroom. Professional development needs are identified by the faculty and training occurs at the school. Administrators monitor the effective use of new skills.

SUMMARY

- The Continuous Improvement System, when implemented as intended, can enhance teacher performance and elevate student achievement in any school.
- Leaders of organizations need a variety of tools to address the myriad issues they face.

- Learning to use the tools created by Glasser, Hall, Herzberg, Lezotte, and Senge will enhance the skills of any organizational leader.
- Throughout the book, I have used the example of a person in the professional setting of an elementary school principal; however, the tools that you will learn to use in this book are applicable to any profession and in any personal relationship.

Before we begin exploring the tools of leadership, consider these statements:

> Leadership is the ability to accurately perceive the present and then influence the future.

> Not every person in a successful organization has the ability to be an effective leader. However, all successful organizations have effective leaders at every level of the organization.

YOUR TASK

At the end of each chapter you will find a space that has been left blank for you to use as you read the book. Your first task will be to carefully describe an individual with whom you are familiar and feel may be struggling with some aspect of his or her life. Don't take a great deal of time to select this person. Go with the first person that comes to mind. You should not identify the person by name.

Describe the person in sufficient detail so that anyone, even a stranger, will feel as if they are very familiar with the person. As you do so, consider:

- Why did this person come to mind?
- How do you think this person feels about him- or herself?
- How would you describe this person's outlook on life?
- If you were assigned to work with this person on an important project, do you believe this person would seek to collaborate and be a productive partner?
- How does this person respond to change?

- Does this person demonstrate a desire to "be the best he (or she) can be"?
- Does this person understand how his or her behavior impacts other individuals?

These questions are only intended to start your thinking about this person. You do not need to answer each question. Feel free to add any other detail that would allow someone to feel as if they know the person you are describing.

_____
_____
_____
_____

1

✣

Is Your School Effective?

Dr. Lawrence Lezotte, "Effective Schools: Past, Present, and Future"

Photo 1.1. Dr. Lawrence Lezotte. Printed by permission of Dr. Lawrence Lezotte.

This chapter is important for two reasons. First, it defines what schools should be in terms of both quality and equity, and second, the Effective Schools Correlates form the foundation of the Continuous Improvement System. While these correlates are specific to schools, I believe that they are also applicable in other environments. After you read the description of each correlate, ask yourself, "If I were the CEO of an organization, would I want the condition described in this correlate present and active in my organization?"

In July of 1966, J. S. Coleman published *The Equality of Educational Opportunity Study*. Coleman's report concluded that a child's success in school was predetermined by the parents' level of education, socioeconomic status, and race. He further asserted that "when it comes to the education of minority and poor children, regardless of the instruction provided, schools don't make a difference." This report led to a multitude of programs intended to improve our educational system and provide services to all students who were struggling to learn.

Educational researchers Dr. Ron Edmonds of Harvard University and Drs. Wilber Brookover and Lawrence Lezotte of Michigan State University quickly questioned Coleman's conclusion and began a quest to find schools that were making a difference in children's lives. Their goal was to identify what was happening in those high-achieving schools but not happening in the low-achieving schools.

As their research progressed, they reached a disturbing conclusion about the American educational system, and Dr. Lezotte discussed it in his paper prepared for the Brock Symposium. "The current system of public education, while designed to provide *access* to all students, was never designed or even intended to *successfully teach* all students a demanding curriculum."

In their review of schools, Brookover, Edmonds, and Lezotte found that when schools are equated based on the clientele they serve, some schools distinguished themselves as having higher levels of student achievement across the board. The success of these schools led to the *learning for all* mission that is the hallmark of effective schools.

With consideration to the success of these schools, Lezotte and his colleagues offered the following definition of an effective school:

> The effective school is a school that can, in outcome terms, demonstrate the presence of equity in the quality of student achievement.

In simple terms, this means that the school as a whole is able to produce evidence of high levels of academic achievement (quality) and evidence that individual students, regardless of their background, are achieving at the same high level (equity).

THE EFFECTIVE SCHOOLS CORRELATES

The research model Lezotte and his colleagues employed involved finding pairs of schools that were in similar geographic environments and with similar socioeconomic, cultural, and family demographics but exhibiting differing levels of student achievement. Conditions that were consistently present in the high-achieving schools but not present in the low-achieving schools were identified. These conditions became known as the Effective Schools Correlates.

The correlates, identified in the original research, have remained consistent through many years of continued research and have served as the foundation of school improvement plans for a multitude of schools. As schools successfully applied the concepts imbedded in the correlates, a second generation of the correlates emerged. The second generation of correlates cannot be successfully implemented until the first generation is firmly in place.

Clear and Focused Mission

(First Generation) There is a clearly articulated mission through which the faculty shares an understanding of and commitment to the instructional priorities, achievement goals, assessment procedures, and accountability. The faculty accepts the responsibility for students' learning the essential curricular priorities.

(Second Generation) There is a shift toward a balance between higher-level learning and the basic skills that are the prerequisites required to attain mastery.

The first generation emphasized teaching for learning for all, while the second generation focused on the learning for all mission.

(Critical Concept) When people understand what must be accomplished and come together in their commitment to achieving that goal, the potential for achieving the goal is greatly enhanced.

Climate of High Expectations for Success

(First Generation) There is a climate of expectation in which the faculty believes that all students can attain mastery of the essential skills present in the curriculum and that they (the faculty, individually and collectively) have the capability to assist all students to achieve that mastery.

(Second Generation) The expectations are launched from a platform that requires educators to apply the same high expectations to self. Educators hold themselves and their colleagues accountable to consistently exhibit their highest level of performance.

(Critical Concept) The people of an organization must be as demanding of themselves as they are of others. The focus must shift from the production effort to the quality of the end product.

Instructional Leadership

(First Generation) The principal acts as the instructional leader. The principal effectively and persistently communicates the mission to the faculty, students, parents, and the extended community.

(Second Generation) The role of leadership is expanded to include members of the faculty. A team of educators, facilitated by the principal, exercises leadership by creating a community driven by shared values. This requires the principal to develop and refine the skills of collaborator, coach, monitor, and cheerleader.

(Critical Concept) The demands of leadership are so great that no individual, working alone, can effectively meet them. When a trusting and respectful relationship is established among colleagues it becomes evident that a small group working together on a complicated issue will produce more and better possible solutions than will any one person working alone.

Opportunity to Learn and Student Time on Task

(First Generation) A high percentage of classroom time is devoted to teacher-led, whole-class instruction focused on the mastery of the high-priority skills. The predominant issue faced by teachers is too much content and too little time.

(Second Generation) The issue of too much to teach and too little time will be addressed by a process of organized abandonment. Educators must be prepared to declare that some things are more important than others and be willing to abandon the lesser important curriculum. The only other option is to significantly increase the amount of time students spend on task. The concept is broadened to include teachers' opportunity to learn through targeted professional development.

(Critical Concept) Organizations and, thus, the people within the organization must recognize "what we do," focus on that, and not dilute the effort by taking on more than can effectively be accomplished.

Frequent Monitoring of Student Progress

(First Generation) The academic progress of students is measured frequently and the information is used to improve the instructional program and to elevate individual student performance.

(Second Generation) The focus shifts from the behavior of the teacher to students monitoring their own progress and making adjustments in their learning practices as they seek to become more successful. A second major change will be a shift away from standardized norm-referenced measures to more authentic assessments of student work, including student products, portfolios, and demonstrated performance.

(Critical Concept) First, people must learn to monitor and manage their own performance and second, performance assessments must move away from paper and pencil "regurgitation" to real-world applications.

Safe and Orderly Environment

(First Generation) The atmosphere in the school is orderly, purposeful, and businesslike. The school environment is free from physical and psychological threat. The overall climate is conducive to teaching and learning.

(Second Generation) The emphasis shifts from working to eliminate undesirable behaviors to working to instill desirable behaviors. Among these are students helping students and educators helping educators.

(Critical Concept) Everyone produces at a higher level when they feel safe and supported in their working environment.

Home–School Relations

(First Generation) Parents understand and support the school's basic mission and have the opportunity to assist the school to achieve that mission.

(Second Generation) A functioning partnership has been forged between the school and the home. Teachers and parents alike accept that they have the same goal—a school where students are safe and respected and achieve at high academic levels.

(Critical Concept) People who are charged with producing a product must be both accessible and responsive to those who consume the product.

DEEPEN YOUR UNDERSTANDING

On the following page, you will find a list of the components of the Continuous Improvement System on the left and on the right a list of the Effective Schools Correlates. Having now read descriptions of the CIS components and the Effective Schools Correlates, draw connecting lines between the components and the correlates that you see as having a relationship. Two obvious connections are depicted as examples.

In your search for relationships, consider how the opportunity to learn correlate relates to the professional development component and how the frequent monitoring correlate relates to the real-time data component.

As you read the remainder of the book, keep these relationships in mind. I'm sure that you will continue to find relationships and, in so doing, you will deepen your understanding of both the Continuous Improvement System and the Effective Schools Correlates.

There are a couple of questions that have long been associated with the Effective Schools Correlates. Principals often ask, "I understand the concepts behind the correlates and want those conditions to exist in my school, but how do I create them?" Researchers ask, "Can you replicate

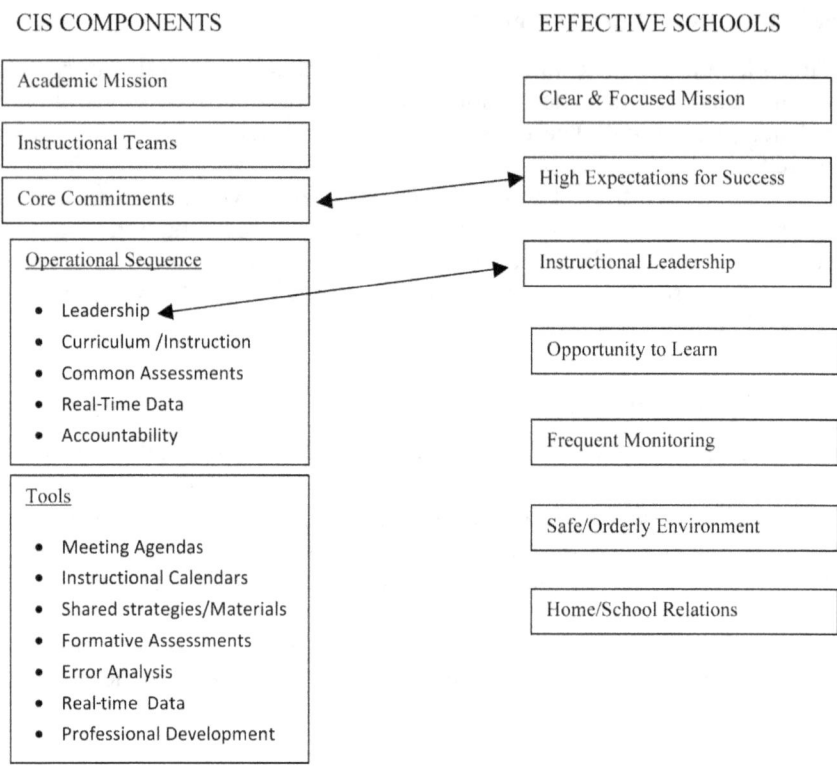

Figure 1.1.

these conditions in multiple schools?" I now firmly believe that implementing the Continuous Improvement System provides answers to both questions. When implemented with fidelity, the CIS moves the correlates from the conceptual to hands-on practices and procedures that can be implemented in any school. Dr. Lezotte has often told me, "You have operationalized the concept."

The data in table 1.1 is from the Arizona Department of Education and reflects work with schools in the early days of concentrating in the Phoenix, Arizona, area. This clearly demonstrates that the system was successfully implemented in multiple schools.

SARGE'S STORY

NOTE: Throughout this story, you will find references to me personally because it is written from my perspective. Whenever you see my name, I

Table 1.1. Impact of the Continuous Improvement System

School	Project Began	Prior Year Aims		Project Ended	Project End Year Aims	
		Math	Reading		Math	Reading
B.A.B. School	February 2007	62	49	May 2008	77	61
C.W. School	June 2007	43	41	April 2010**	73	72
A.F.G. School	August 2005*	53	45	May 2009	54	49
A.M.H. School	December 2006	27	31	May 2009	65	65
J.L.K. School	October 2005*	48	42	May 2009	59	62
M. School	June 2007	57	54	April 2010**	66	66
O. School	August 2006	51	52	May 2009	67	59
O.W. School	November 2008	51	52	Ongoing**	60	63
S. B. School	October 2008	42	46	Ongoing**	60	52
W.R.S. School	October 2006	41	34	May 2009	57	50
W. School	August 2006	40	40	May 2009	67	58

* The Arizona Department of Education changed math and reading tests between the 2004 and the 2005 school year, therefore the score reported is from the end of the first year of the project.
** The Arizona Department of Education changed the math test for the 2010 school year, therefore the score reported is from the final year of the 2005–2009 test.

encourage you to replace my name with yours. Put yourself into the situation and determine how the tools fit for you.

Several years ago, I was contacted by the superintendent of a small metropolitan school district and asked to work with an elementary school principal who was in trouble at his school. The superintendent told me that the principal, whom I will call Mr. Alan Wilson, was a former marine and the superintendent's respect for those who serve our country in the military played a large role in his decision to hire Mr. Wilson (Sarge). The superintendent explained that he felt that, as a marine, when Sarge was given an order by a superior, he would respond immediately and with vigor, and he was having difficulty understanding why the faculty at his school did not respond to him in the same way. The conversations that are related in Sarge's story are my best recollections and not direct quotes.

> Dr. S.: Before we begin our discussion, I want to assure you that your superintendent has asked me to come here as a friend and colleague and not as an evaluator to report on your job performance.
>
> Sarge: Yeah, that's what he told me, too. We'll see how this works out.
>
> Dr. S.: I know that it will take some time to earn your trust but I will work very hard to do just that.
>
> Sarge: OK, let's get on with it. What do you want to know?

Dr. S.: Tell me a bit about yourself. I know you came from a distinguished military background. That is not a typical path to an elementary school principalship. What brought you here?

Sarge: My college degree was in elementary education but after I got involved in ROTC I decided to make the military my career. I gained the rank of sergeant major very quickly and was held in high esteem by my base commander. Two years ago, I got married and we have a little girl. My wife decided that she did not want to raise our daughter in the military environment. When my hitch was up, I resigned and applied for jobs in education.

Dr. S.: How do you feel about your decision to leave the military? Has the transition from military life to civilian life been difficult for you?

Sarge: To be honest, civilian life seems very chaotic. I do miss the order of the military.

Dr. S.: After a month on the job, how do you feel things are going here?

Sarge: Obviously things are not going well here or you wouldn't be sitting in my office.

Dr. S.: I asked a couple of teachers for directions to your office and noted that they referred to you as Sarge and not Principal Wilson. How do you feel about that?

Sarge: It does remind them who gives the orders here, so I like it.

Dr. S.: If it's OK with you, I'll call you Alan. Tell me about your relationship with the faculty.

Sarge: These people are malcontents and whiners! When I give an order, the first thing they do is question me and then go running to the superintendent.

Dr. S.: Tell me about one of those times.

Sarge: When the superintendent sent me here he ordered me to do whatever I had to do to raise the level of student achievement. At the end of the day, I watched teachers' cars follow the buses out of the parking lot. This was a long-standing practice. I sent a memo to each teacher that they had to sign and return to me. The memo ordered them to hold a forty-five-minute tutor session after dismissal for any child who was behind. They filed a complaint with the superintendent and he ruled for the teachers. Now whenever I want to do anything, I have to run it by the superintendent first and get his permission. No one shows respect for the chain of command or for wanting to do what is needed!

Dr. S.: When you arrived here, how did you communicate the mission you had been given by the superintendent?

Sarge: I called a faculty meeting and told everyone what I had been sent here to do and that they either needed to get on board or find a new school.

Dr. S.: How did the faculty respond?

Sarge: I told you, they responded like the malcontents and whiners that they are.

Dr. S.: Is there some other way that you could have approached this mission issue?

Sarge: Yeah, I guess so. I could have gone through some touchy-feely goal-setting stuff, but I already knew how it had to come out, so why waste the time?

Dr. S.: How are you monitoring progress toward your goal?

Sarge: Every Wednesday I walk through every classroom on campus. I know who is doing their job!

Dr. S.: This may give you a bit of insight into teacher performance, but how do you know if the students are actually learning what they are supposed to learn?

Sarge: I'll know when we get the results of the first semester benchmark test.

Dr. S.: How will you know if the students are prepared for the semester test?

Sarge: That is the teachers' job, and those kids better be ready or there will be consequences.

Dr. S.: Alan, I have to be honest with you. You are creating an environment that is preventing you from, not helping you to, accomplish your mission. I can change that for you. I can give you a system and teach you how to use it if you will trust me and cooperate. Will you do that?

Sarge: It looks like if I want to keep my job I'll have to. Get on with it. Tell me what to do.

Dr. S.: There are several things that you will have to do as we begin. You need to carefully read literature I will give to you on the effective schools research. You need to call at least two of the people on this list and talk to them about their experience with the Continuous Improvement System. You need to carefully explore the website noted at the bottom of the page. You will have to visit a school with me where the CIS is successfully functioning. After you do all that, you will have to spend at least a half day with me learning about the CIS. When I'm confident that you understand the CIS, you will have to meet with me on a frequent and continual basis so I can teach you how to implement the system and give you feedback on your decisions and the impact of those decisions. Will you do that?

Sarge: I'm willing to do whatever will save my job, and the system thing sounds interesting.

Sarge did everything that he agreed to do and learned a considerable amount about effective schools and the CIS. It was evident that there was not only a need to change Sarge's behavior but also a need to change the structure and culture of the school. I decided to use a foundation of knowledge of the Effective Schools Correlates and implementing the CIS to accomplish this.

It has long been my practice to use a mind map process to create a visual image of a complicated situation. The map is, in a sense, my lesson plan. A mind map depicts a system in that it combines multiple components into a complex whole and demonstrates how the components interact.

This process makes it possible to see all the different factors involved in the situation and the forces that are being brought to bear on them. The first phase of the mind map that was used with Sarge appears on the following page in figure 1.2.

Additions to the mind map will appear near the end of each chapter.

This first phase of my mind map depicted the following:

- Sarge's behavior was having a significant negative impact on the organizational structure and culture of the school.
- Sarge showed interest in the relationship between the Effective Schools Correlates and the Continuous Improvement System and indicated a desire to implement the CIS.
- The implementation of the CIS was the most efficient and effective way to influence both Sarge's behavior and the organizational structure and culture of the school.
- Sarge's knowledge of leading a school was very limited, and it would be necessary for me to act as both a role model and coach.

SUMMARY

- Some schools that serve similar populations produce higher levels of academic achievement than others.
- The conditions that exist in these schools but do not exist in lower-performing schools have been identified and are known as the Effective Schools Correlates.
- The concepts that are set forth in the correlates have been transformed into hands-on practical procedures in the Continuous Improvement System.
- When implemented with fidelity, the CIS has a powerful impact on both teacher and student performance.
- The CIS can successfully be replicated in multiple schools.

> A quote from Dr. Edmonds provides a fitting conclusion to this chapter. "We can, whenever and wherever we choose, successfully teach all children whose schooling is of interest to us. We already know more than we need to do that. Whether or not we do it must finally depend on how we feel about the fact that we haven't done it so far."

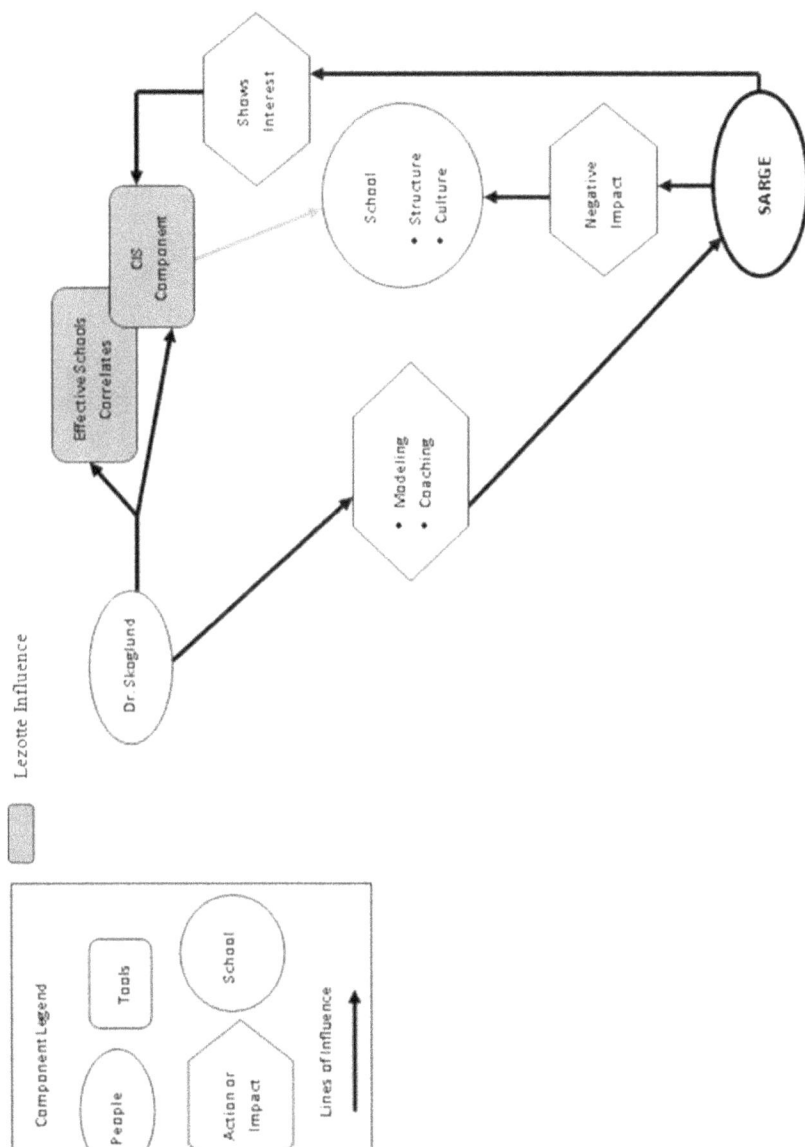

Figure 1.2.

YOUR TASK

Determine which of the Effective Schools Correlates you believe is most important for Sarge to understand. Develop a "lesson plan" for how you would teach this correlate to Sarge and then develop a plan to create the condition embodied in the correlate in the school.

_____
_____
_____
_____

2

✣

Meeting Our Basic Needs
Dr. William Glasser, Control Theory

Photo 2.1. Dr. William Glasser. Printed by permission of Dr. William Glasser.

Now that we have reviewed the basics of the effective schools research and how it serves as the foundation of the Continuous Improvement System, it is time to focus on the people who will be called upon to implement the CIS.

In his best-selling book, *Control Theory*, Dr. Glasser asserts that all humans have a core of basic psychological needs that drive our behavior. These needs are at the very core of our being and we spend our entire lives continually seeking to satisfy them. Among the most powerful basic psychological needs that continually impact our personal and professional relationships are the following:

- The need to *belong*. We have a need to love and to be loved. We need to feel that we are accepted in a family, by friends, or in a work group. We need to feel worthy and to have our self-esteem affirmed.
- The need for *freedom*. We have a need to choose how we live our lives, to choose those with whom we form relationships, to choose to

move about without restriction, and to choose to form our own beliefs and to openly express our thoughts. Our country was founded as a place where people could live in this way. Worldwide, many have given their lives in a fight to obtain, or to preserve, freedom.
- The need for *fun*. We have a need to play and enjoy life. We enjoy playing games, especially if the game is with a child and we covertly allow the child to win. It is natural for us to seek others to share in the experiences that bring us joy. If a white-water raft trip is on your "to do" list, I assure you, even if you do it alone, you will find it exhilarating. However, if you do this in the company of a friend, the experience will be enhanced.
- The need for *power*. We have a need to exert ourselves over other people, the task at hand, and our environment. We seek to have other people do as we direct or behave as we want them to behave. This need develops very early. A clear example of this can frequently be seen by observing two young siblings interact. We exercise our need for power when we compete with others for promotions on the job. We build and operate machines in order to perform tasks more efficiently and effectively. We include many appliances and furniture items in our homes to create a comfortable environment. How often have you heard someone say, "I hate it when the machine is smarter than I am!" Such a statement is an indication that the person has lost control of the situation and now feels a need to exercise power in an attempt to regain control. There may be no greater sense of frustration or pain than that which we experience when we feel that we are not in control of our lives.

It is perfectly natural for us to attempt to make our environment what we want it to be. When we get into a car in July, it is hot inside the car and we turn on the air conditioner to make the environment comfortable. This is an example of an accepted use of power. It is true that some individuals respond to this need in ways that are inappropriate. History is replete with examples of individuals who responded to their need for power by conquering others and shedding the blood of millions of people in the process.

Dr. Glasser states that these needs are "encoded in our genes." They are present at birth and remain with us throughout our lives. They are interwoven. Some are compatible but there are times when our needs conflict with each other. Our needs to belong and to have fun are very compatible. Consider the following examples from different stages of our lives.

Babies exhibit joy with every fiber of their being. Watch what happens when an infant is picked up from the crib, held gently, and tickled. The infant's needs to feel loved and to experience fun are immediately met.

Look carefully at the faces of teenage athletes as they leave the football field following the championship game. It will not be difficult to determine which team won. We all know that it is much more fun to win. Competition is about power. When power is involved, fun is negatively impacted for at least one of the competitors. It is highly likely that both teams will gather and remind themselves that they will always belong to the team.

As an adult, I played golf every Saturday morning for many years with the same foursome. We always had some type of side game that usually had the winner collecting the huge sum of twenty-five cents from each of the other players after each hole. Money was never an issue because this was not about a competition to win money. It was about being with a group of friends and playing a game we enjoyed.

The desire for power is frequently the origin of conflict. How often have we seen children act out because they feel the rules set down by their parents have curtailed their freedom and ability to have fun? History has recorded many examples of people rebelling against a dictator or a government that had deprived them of their freedom. Our desire to have others believe what we believe or act as we want them to act often conflicts with their need to belong, to be accepted for who they are, to be free, and to exert their own need for power.

As adults, we frequently exert our power over our children in an effort to protect them. They may be better served if we stop making decisions for them and teach them to make good choices. In doing this, suggest the following to a youth who is struggling with a decision. If you are trying to decide if you should do something, ask yourself: Would I be excited to come home and tell my parents about it? If the answer is yes, then choosing to do it is probably a good decision. If you would not want your parents to know what you had done, then choosing to do it is probably a bad decision.

Life is a never-ending series of choices. As we grow older, the choices come at us faster, the situations become more complicated, and the consequences of the choices we make become greater. The quality of the choices that we make will determine the quality of life that we experience. When we choose successful/effective behaviors, we choose a happier life. We can also choose to change behaviors that thwart our ability to meet our basic psychological needs.

We each carry within us a "picture" of how we want life to be. We constantly compare that picture with our perceived reality. When there is a significant difference between the two, we are driven to take some action to resolve the conflict. The action we take is the result of our own conscious decisions. Our behavior is *not* controlled by external forces! Glasser states, "Absent mental impairment, our behavior is a matter of choice!"

When someone exhibits a behavior that creates a strong feeling within us, we must accept two facts: (1) we cannot control our feelings—we experience them. However, we can control the behavior that we exhibit in response to those feelings; and (2) we cannot control the other person's behavior. Only they may choose to change their behavior.

As an example, suppose a coworker has a habit of tapping a pen on the desk. You may choose to respond by allowing this to annoy you, to distract you and impact the quality of your work. You may choose to get angry and yell at the person. In doing so, you have chosen to lose your control over your environment and negatively impact the coworker's need to belong. Such a choice will not resolve the problem. You chose this behavior—the coworker did not force you to respond in this way. You could have made a choice to respond to your feelings by thinking about how to more successfully approach the coworker. "I noticed that you tap your pen on the desk when you are thinking through a problem. You may not even be aware of it, but it makes it difficult for me to concentrate on the problem I have before me. Would you be kind enough to tap the pen against your leg so there will be no sound to distract me?"

As leaders of organizations, or as friends, we can learn to recognize that the negative behavior exhibited by others is the result of one or more of the basic psychological needs going unmet. With this knowledge, we can help people to understand what is missing in their lives, how their current behavior may be the source of their problems, and assist them to make better behavioral choices. This is a powerful tool to have in your toolbox.

SARGE'S STORY

Dr. S.: Have you read the literature I gave you about the effective schools research and the Continuous Improvement System?

Sarge: Yes I have, and I really liked the CIS stuff. It reminded me of military organization. It gave me the impression that if we did it, I would be able to figure out what was really going on in the school.

Dr. S.: You and I still need to do some studying before we start to implement the CIS. Do you have any ideas of how you would go about implementing it?

Sarge: Yes. I would have you explain it to everyone and then I would give everyone one week to put everything in place or face the consequences.

Dr. S.: That "here are your marching orders" approach did not seem to be well accepted when you informed the faculty of the mission you were sent here to accomplish. Do you expect it to produce different results this time?

Sarge: No, I suppose not. I'm sure that you have a plan. What is it?

Dr. S.: I do have a plan to suggest, but first let's consider why you are getting this resistive response from the faculty. Remember, you are in a civilian setting now. People just naturally resist change, and being told what to do is a change here. People especially don't like being told what to do when they have no input and feel that they may know more than the person giving the orders. Is that a fair assessment of what is happening here?

Sarge: Yeah, I understand, and the teachers understand that they know more than I do about teaching kids.

Dr. S.: OK, will you trust me to do some things that will put you in better standing with the faculty and create a better opportunity for a successful implementation of the CIS?

Sarge: Yeah, like I said, I'll do whatever I have to do to save my job.

Dr. S.: Do you like being around the kids?

Sarge: This is not how I remember school. These kids are unmotivated and very undisciplined. What makes it even worse is their parents support their lack of effort and poor behavior.

Dr. S.: Is there anything that happens during a normal day that you particularly enjoy?

Sarge: Yes, locking the door at 4:00 p.m. and going home.

Dr. S.: I appreciate your candor. We are scheduled to meet again in ten days; however, if it is OK with you, I may drop by a few additional times to toss around some ideas.

Sarge: Yes sir, just give me a heads-up that you are on the way and I'll make time for you.

Following this and several consequent conversations, some things became very clear to me. In baseball terms, Sarge was 0–4 in meeting his basic psychological needs. He was neither accepted nor respected by the faculty. The superintendent had taken away his freedom to do his job as he saw fit. He most certainly was not having any fun. It was his inappropriate use of power (control) that was having a negative impact in other areas. There was far too much going on here to "fix" everything at once. In creating a plan to work together, I made the decision to first focus on his control issues. Sarge needed badly to understand the difference between the military culture and the culture in a civilian elementary school. His decision to continue to act as he did in the military was destroying his chance of being a successful principal, and he needed to make better decisions in order to change his behavior and adapt to his new environment. I knew that this would be no easy task. Forfeiting some amount of power in order to become more successful is a very difficult concept for many people to grasp.

I saw Sarge as being trapped by his own poor decisions and corresponding behaviors. I identified his need for power as the primary source of the conflicts within and surrounding Sarge.

His need for power was clearly conflicting with his needs (1) to be accepted and respected by the faculty, (2) to be granted the freedom to do his job as he saw fit, and (3) to be enjoying his transition into a new culture. We were fortunate to have a large military base located nearby. In discussions with the superintendent, I learned that two retired officers lived in his community and he frequently played golf with them. We requested and received their assistance. The superintendent invited Sarge to complete a foursome for golf the next weekend. This social activity opened the door for discussing the difference between military and civilian life and the need to adapt to the new environment. The two men did not formally counsel Sarge, they simply related their experiences, the difficulty they had adjusting to civilian life, and the changes in both thinking and behavior that they had to make as they transitioned to civilian life.

I asked Sarge if there was anyone on the faculty that he respected and trusted. He identified one veteran teacher—Jim. I carefully prepped Jim before including him in meetings with Sarge. Sarge gave him permission to "speak freely" and he did so with clarity but no animosity. His description of how Sarge's behavior made him feel was a real eye-opener for Sarge. As a result, Sarge agreed to treat him with more respect and to do the same with all teachers.

During the next ten days, I met with Sarge frequently. Our conversations focused on his need to control every aspect of the school and the reaction of the teachers when he issued orders. I did explain the basic psychological need of power to him and talked at length about how his behavior was impacting all the people around him. We candidly discussed how it made the people feel toward him and how their feelings were impacting him. He started with the typical, "I don't care if people like me. I'm here to do a job." From there we assessed how his behavior was interfering with his opportunity to accomplish that job. Having to face the fact that no progress was being made and acknowledge the less-than-positive feedback he was receiving from other sources, Sarge agreed to enter into a dialogue with me concerning what he needed to change and how to make the change.

I continually pressed him to look at how his decision to deal with the teachers only from a position of power was working out for him. In a few situations, he conceded that a more collaborative approach could have produced better results. This was a small sign that he was becoming aware of how his decisions were inhibiting progress toward his charge of increasing the level of student achievement in the school.

Meeting Our Basic Needs 19

The new phase of the map depicts Sarge's need for power conflicting with his other basic psychological needs and those of the faculty. The inappropriate behavior resulting from his need for power was having a very negative impact on the psychological needs of the faculty in that they felt their power had been stripped, their freedom to teach as they desired was restricted, and the relationship with Sarge was not fun. His behavior was clearly having a negative impact on the school's ability to accomplish the academic mission and on his role as a leader.

It appeared that the introduction of three factors offered the best opportunity to have a positive influence on Sarge's need for power. Those

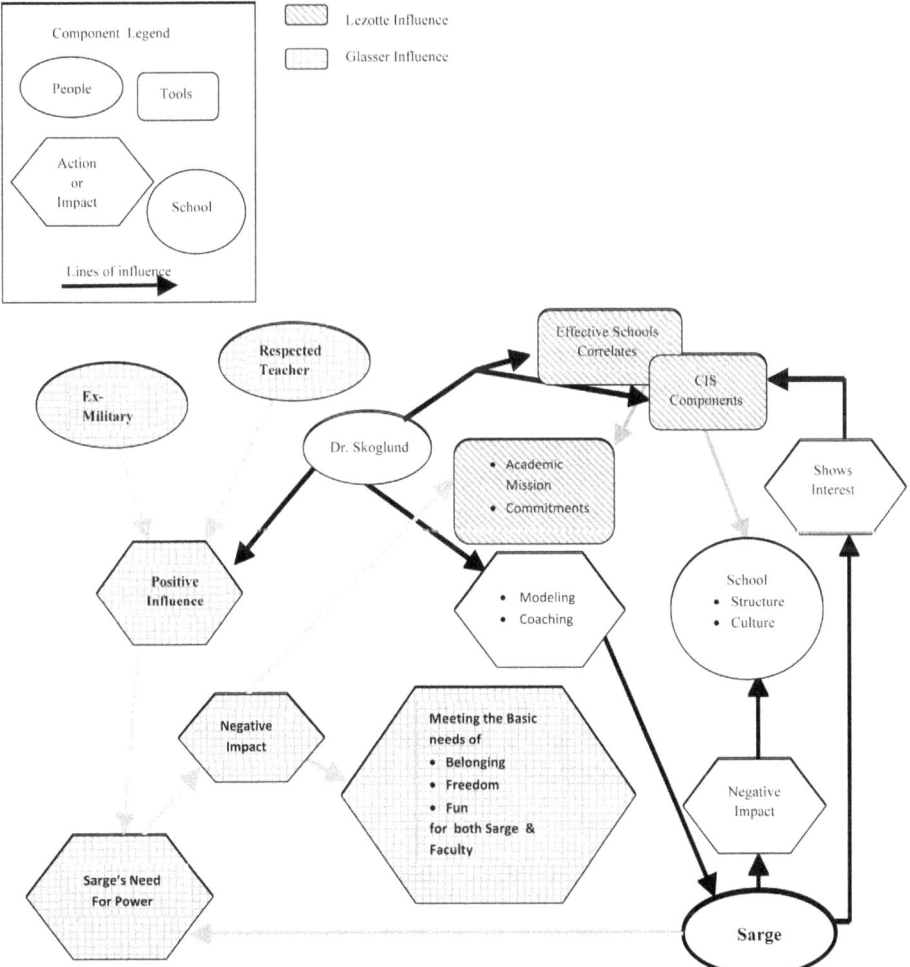

Figure 2.1.

factors were (1) my counsel, (2) the insight of a respected teacher, and (3) a relationship with ex-military personnel.

Mind maps do become complicated. In order to make the progression of my mind map easy for you to follow, new sections are shown in a new pattern. Sarge's need for power had been identified as having a negative impact on the school structure and culture. The new section depicts the impact of his need for power on the other basic psychological needs desired by both him and the faculty. This also interfered with the process of the faculty identifying the academic mission and the core commitments. Three factors were now being introduced to exert a positive influence and assist Sarge in dealing with his need for power and the negative impact that was the result.

SUMMARY

- Human behavior is driven by our desire to satisfy our basic psychological needs.
- We make conscious choices as to how we go about meeting these needs.
- The quality of the choices we make dictates the quality of life we experience.
- We have the ability to choose to eliminate behaviors that are not successful in meeting our psychological needs.
- Our behaviors have an impact on those around us and their responses have, in turn, an impact on us.
- Paying attention to these needs can help us understand a person's behavior and appropriately respond to that behavior.

YOUR TASK

Analyze the person you described at the end of the introduction chapter with consideration to the basic psychological needs discussed in this chapter. Has this information on some of our basic needs helped you to better understand the person?

_____
_____
_____

3

Don't Forget Your Change!

*Dr. Gene Hall, Implementing Change:
Patterns, Principles, and Potholes*

Photo 3.1. Dr. Gene Hall. Printed by permission of Dr. Gene Hall.

Change is a very personal experience. While some individuals are adventuresome and demonstrate excitement about exploring new experiences, they are in the minority. It is a very normal reaction for us to resist change. Status quo is usually a very comfortable place for most people and so they are often reluctant to move away from familiar thought and behavior patterns.

One can choose to make, or accept, a change in one's personal life quickly (remember, behavior is a matter of choice). Bringing about changes in policy and procedure in an organization is much more complicated and usually cannot be effectively accomplished quickly. The size of the organization is obviously a factor in the change process but the need to allow time for the change to become ingrained is a consistent requirement in every organization. Dr. Hall is often quoted as saying, "Change is a process, not an event." It may take from three to five years for a significant change to become fully ingrained in a large organization. Attempts to force the change at a faster pace will almost always result in increased resistance.

Attempts to bring change to organizations have often failed because the focus was on the change itself with little attention being paid to the people who were expected to implement the change. It is of vital importance that the focus of the change facilitator(s) is on the people first and the change second!

When change is introduced into a person's life, it is natural for that person to experience concern. Successful change facilitators recognize that the person will experience difficulty in accepting the change until the concern is addressed.

Dr. Hall has, over many years, studied the impact of change on people in many professional settings and in multiple countries and cultures. The result of each study was the identification of a set of broad concerns that were common to all people as they faced significant change. These findings led to the creation of the Concerns-Based Adoption Model (CBAM). Through this model, Dr. Hall offers change facilitators tools to identify the concern(s) people are experiencing and some possible interventions that will address the concern(s) and allow the person to move on.

STAGES OF CONCERN

Dr. Hall's research identified seven broad concerns that were experienced by people who were facing change. Because people had to move past the concern they were experiencing before they progressed in their acceptance of the change, the title of "stages of concern" (SOC) was adopted. There was no consistent sequence of concerns that people experienced. In fact, people frequently experienced more than one concern at a time. It was also determined that the stages are not value laden. It is not nobler to experience one concern as opposed to another.

The stages of concern are named and defined in the following. A statement that you might hear from a person experiencing the concern is also provided. (NOTE: The term "innovation" is used to refer to any pending specific change. Change is a broad conceptual term and innovation refers to something specific such as a policy, procedure, practice, or the introduction of new tools.)

Awareness

In this stage, the person exhibits little knowledge of or concern about the innovation. ("I've heard of this but will not worry about it until it actually happens.")

Information

This stage is marked by a general awareness of the innovation. The person is not worried about the personal impact of the innovation. There is an expressed desire by the person to learn more about the general characteristics, effects, and requirements for use, and when the change will take place. ("It sounds like this is going to happen. I will need to know much more before I decide how I feel about it.")

Personal

The person now is questioning what his or her role will be, the demands of the innovation, and his or her own ability to meet those demands. Financial status, social status, and personal/professional relationship issues may also surface in this stage. ("Oh boy, what is this going to do to me?")

Management

The person's attention is now focused on the tasks involved in the use of the innovation. Issues concerning time demands, organization, and efficiency move to the forefront. ("How am I going to do this on top of all I am already doing?")

Consequence

In this stage, the person considers how the innovation will impact the people within his or her immediate sphere of influence. Is the innovation relevant to their work and their ability to accomplish the work? Will additional changes need to be made to successfully implement the innovation? ("This is going to impact my team and I'm worried about exactly how.")

Collaboration

The focus in this stage is on coordination and cooperation with others in relation to the innovation. ("How are you approaching the innovation? Perhaps we should meet and share some ideas.")

Refocusing

People become interested in exploring major changes in the innovation or even replacing the innovation with a more effective alternative. ("I think I have an idea that may be better than what we are now doing.")

Identifying the stage(s) of concern that a person is experiencing is really not all that difficult. You simply have to pay attention to what they are saying.

Identify the stage of concern expressed in each statement by writing the name of the stage on the line to the left of the statement.

1. _____ We really have not been told much about this new procedure so I haven't even thought about it. When I know what is going to be asked of us, then I will have questions.
2. _____ I'm afraid that this new procedure is going to cause problems for me. I'm not sure I can do it and I'm worried about messing it up and jeopardizing my relationship with my colleagues.
3. _____ I think that this new procedure would be better accepted if we met and really talked about what we are expected to do. I'm sure that I would benefit from hearing how others are going to approach it, and I have a couple of ideas I would like to share.
4. _____ This new procedure is very complex and I'm concerned about the impact it will have on my team. The team that I lead is not enthusiastic about it, and I'm not sure I can make them see how this is more effective than our current procedure.
5. _____ If we are to bring new teachers into our schools and have them be effective on day one, we need to improve their college preparation and our own orientation process. Higher education needs to have a better balance between the content and how to teach it. We need to have activities where new teachers must teach in front of the experienced faculty so we can offer constructive feedback.
6. _____ I know that lesson plans are required, but I just don't have time to write detailed plans for three different classes. I'm already buried in papers to be corrected and forms to be filled out for the district office.
7. _____ I'm a new faculty member and I realize there is a lot I don't know about how things work here. I wish there was a handbook of all the procedures that I could read.

The answers are below. Key words have also been identified in each statement that lead you to the identification of the stage of concern.

1. <u>Awareness</u>: Key Words: "have not been told much"; "I haven't even thought about it"
2. <u>Personal</u>: Key Words: "cause problems for me"; "not sure I can do it"
3. <u>Collaboration</u>: Key Words: "if we met"; "benefit from hearing how others are going to approach it"; "ideas I would like to share"
4. <u>Consequence</u>: Key Words: "impact it will have on my team"; "make them see how this is more effective"

5. <u>Refocusing</u>: Key Words: "need to improve their college preparation and our own orientation"
6. <u>Management</u>: Key Words: "I just don't have time"
7. <u>Information</u>: Key Words: "I realize there is a lot I don't know"; "I wish there was a handbook"

Engaging people in dialogue is an effective method of hearing their concerns firsthand. This does require the facilitator to make judgments quickly. There are times when you will want significant time to analyze the statements people are making. In these situations it is helpful to ask people to respond in writing. Give people an open-ended prompt and allow them time to think through what they are really feeling. (EXAMPLE: When I think about the new innovation, I am concerned about . . .)

INTERVENTIONS

The concerns that people experience when facing change inhibit their ability to accept the change. When a person is concerned that an innovation may demand skills that the person does not possess and therefore the person's career may be threatened, he or she will not typically embrace the change until the concern is addressed to the person's satisfaction.

Once the stage of concern the person is experiencing is identified, the focus must shift to helping the person move through that stage of concern and toward acceptance of the change. It is vital to understand that the person cannot be forced, tricked, or dragged kicking and screaming through a stage of concern. The feelings associated with the stage must be faced and addressed. Only then will the person move on to experience new concerns or embrace the change.

On the following pages you will find suggested interventions for each stage of concern. These are not the only interventions. Do not make intervening too complicated. If you are not sure what to do, ask the person, "What would alleviate your concern?" Remember, the goal is to remove the person's concern and assist the person to move ahead.

Possible Interventions for Awareness Concerns

- Share enough information to arouse interest
- Encourage unaware individuals to talk with colleagues who know about the innovation
- Relate the innovation to an area that is already of interest to the person
- Involve people in dialogue and decisions as the innovation is implemented

- Minimize speculation by providing timely and accurate information
- Announce that the innovation is being implemented and is required

Possible Interventions for Collaboration Concerns

- Provide training and opportunity for people to work in collaborative situations
- Allow people to share how they are approaching the innovation in meetings and allow time for questions and dialogue
- Provide the same pertinent information to all members of a work group
- Meet with groups whose work is related and discuss how they can assist each other

Possible Interventions for Consequence Concerns

- Meet with these people frequently and discuss how things are going for them
- Discuss the impact of the innovation on the work they are charged to accomplish
- Discuss the personal and professional impact of the innovation on the person
- Ask the leader of a group to identify what is needed to have the group embrace the innovation and make it effective for them

Possible Interventions for Information Concerns

- Don't overlook the obvious. Ask people what they feel they need to know and then provide that specific information
- Detail the difference between what currently exists and what will exist when the innovation is implemented
- Fully explain any new demands that will be made on the people
- Explain, in great detail, the benefits that will be derived from the innovation
- Arrange for groups to visit other organizations where the innovation has been implemented and have the group report on what they learned

Possible Interventions for Management Concerns

- Demonstrate practical solutions to logistical issues
- Give people opportunities to practice with the innovation prior to implementation and collaborate to find solutions to the issues that arise

- Demonstrate how the requirements of the innovation relate to what people are already doing
- Eliminate some of the tasks that are of lesser importance to allow time for the innovation

Possible Interventions for Personal Concerns

- Acknowledge that it is OK to have these feelings. They are natural and normal
- Connect these individuals with others who have experienced and resolved similar issues
- Establish "dialogue groups" where people can discuss their concerns and how to address them
- Don't push—act as a caring colleague

Possible Interventions for Refocusing Concerns

- Make it clear that ideas to improve the innovation or ideas to replace the innovation with something more effective are invited and will be considered
- Talk with people and help them to clarify their ideas
- Assist these individuals to access the resources they need to fully develop their idea
- Keep these individuals focused on positive contributions and avoid allowing them to become disruptive

Remember to use common sense when responding to people's concerns. The simplest response is usually the best response.

It is vital to respond with an intervention appropriate to the stage of concern. If a person is stating that he or she is unable to keep up with the demands (a management concern) and then hears "We have to do it for the kids" (a consequence response), the person will feel that he or she has not been listened to and will become more resistant to the innovation!

COMMON ERRORS THAT INHIBIT IMPLEMENTATION OF CHANGE

Dr. Hall reports that there are a significant number of errors made by individuals and organizations as they seek to implement change. Here are the four most common errors:

Underestimating the Power of Vision

Dr. Lezotte discussed the importance of a clear and focused mission in creating an effective school. This concept holds true for any organization. A vision that is known, accepted, and willingly pursued by the people of an organization is a powerful force. Without a vision to guide them, people are left to "do their own thing" and this severely reduces productivity. Creating such a vision requires time and attention to detail. A memo, speech, and some catchy slogans will not produce the vision. The vision must be the topic of frequent dialogues. These dialogues should define the vision and include data that measures progress.

Failing to Create a Powerful Critical Mass

An individual leader, working alone, no matter how competent, charismatic, and dedicated, will rarely be able to overcome the power of the system in place. People's attachment to the status quo is simply too strong. The most effective leaders form coalitions of the power brokers in the organization and gain their support prior to announcing a significant change. These people can act as role models and assist in addressing many individual and collective concerns.

Allowing Established Culture to Block Implementation

The roadblocks that exist within the organization are often associated with such things as policies, paperwork, insufficient training, and a lack of resources and support. Leaders must carefully review current policy and ensure that it is not a point of contention. People always appreciate the elimination of unnecessary paperwork; this demonstrates the organization's respect for people's time. The lack of resources required to successfully implement and use an innovation will lead directly to resistance to the innovation and defense of the status quo.

Failing to Celebrate Short-Term Success

Change takes time and people need to know that progress is being made. It is important for leaders to celebrate every possible small success that occurs. Failure to do this negatively impacts morale because people feel that no one is appreciating their effort. When morale is diminished, momentum is lost. The smart leader will set progress goals that are specific and measurable. Meeting each goal should be a reason for the leader to gather the people of the organization, congratulate them, and perhaps distribute tangible rewards.

Bringing change to a large organization is a significant challenge. It can be done if you keep Dr. Hall's words in mind: "The people must change before the organization will change."

SARGE'S STORY

Time was passing quickly. The students in Sarge's school were hard at work taking the first-quarter benchmark tests and he was nervously awaiting the results.

After over two months of regular dialogue with Sarge, I felt that he was making real progress. If we met on a Monday, I would hear all about the golf game of the just-past Saturday and a few additional stories about the nineteenth hole. Sarge, the two military officers, and their wives had made arrangements for each couple to host a weekly dinner that rotated among the three homes. He often spoke of how helpful they were in assisting him to adjust to civilian life. I observed that he now felt that he belonged to a social group and he was having fun on the golf course.

We spent a great deal of time with the leadership team learning to use the Concerns-Based Adoption Model. The training began with team members interviewing each other and identifying the stage of concern being expressed. The team then engaged in a dialogue to identify the most appropriate intervention. Sarge demonstrated real interest in the CBAM and proved to be a quick learner. We conducted a CBAM conference with each of the instructional teams. Every team expressed management and consequence concerns. With this information, the leadership team was able to design professional development activities that gave the faculty the tools required to be much more efficient in using the system. We also organized cross-grade-level meetings that allowed them to share how they saw the CIS impacting their students. Several teachers asked for additional materials and Sarge quickly provided what they requested. It became obvious to me that the teachers were developing a newfound respect for Sarge.

My next interview with Sarge was very encouraging.

> Dr. S.: Alan, I've noticed a difference in you these past weeks. Are you aware of any changes in your decision making and behavior?
>
> Sarge: I hate to admit it but I seem to be mellowing out a bit.
>
> Dr. S.: I think that's a good description and a positive change. To what do you attribute that?
>
> Sarge: A couple of things—you, my new golfing friends, and the meetings we have been conducting with the leadership team. I feel good that I can

delegate tasks to them and know that they will carry them out. It has taken a lot of pressure off me.

Dr. S.: When we first met, you felt things were not going well here at the school. How do you feel now?

Sarge: I feel much better. I have to admit that I didn't know the first thing about running a school but with the Continuous Improvement System in place, I feel like I'm starting to know what is going on. I know that I still have a lot to learn and I'm finding myself really wanting to learn. The meetings we had with the instructional teams where you used the CBAM to facilitate the dialogue were amazing. Several teachers have made a point to tell me how much they appreciated the opportunity to let me know where the problems were occurring.

Dr. S.: How would you describe your relationship with the faculty today as opposed to the relationship at the start of the year?

Sarge: Oh, it is very different. All the talks with Jim [respected teacher] and my golfing friends have made me aware of how my attempts to employ military tactics were not working out. All that you have taught me about how to run a school and how to listen to people and remove their concerns have made me rethink how I have to approach the job. I'm able to just talk with teachers now and we often jointly decide what to do. I accept that they know a lot more about teaching kids than I do, so most times I just let them do what they want to do. All this has greatly reduced the tension that was there early in the year.

Dr. S.: Alan, I'm really very proud of you. Not everyone would be willing to admit what you just did. I'm pleased with your desire to continue to learn. We will continue to explore the CIS and CBAM and you will become more efficient and effective in using these tools.

Sarge and the leadership team needed to continue to develop as a collaborative and effective unit. The CBAM was the perfect tool to continue developing their relationship and as they did so they became more effective in advancing the use of the CIS. This had an impact on the school's culture as the teachers began to feel that someone was listening to their problems and willing to provide the support they felt they needed.

I added the CBAM component to my mind map. This helped me to maintain a "big picture" view of the general situation and the interaction of the specific components. It was important for me to keep in mind that I not only needed to teach the CBAM to Sarge and the leadership team, but I also needed to direct them in how to use it to advance the CIS.

The new section of the mind map depicts how my teaching the leadership team the skills of using the CBAM had an impact on the school structure and culture and assisted the team to more effectively implement the components of the CIS.

Don't Forget Your Change!

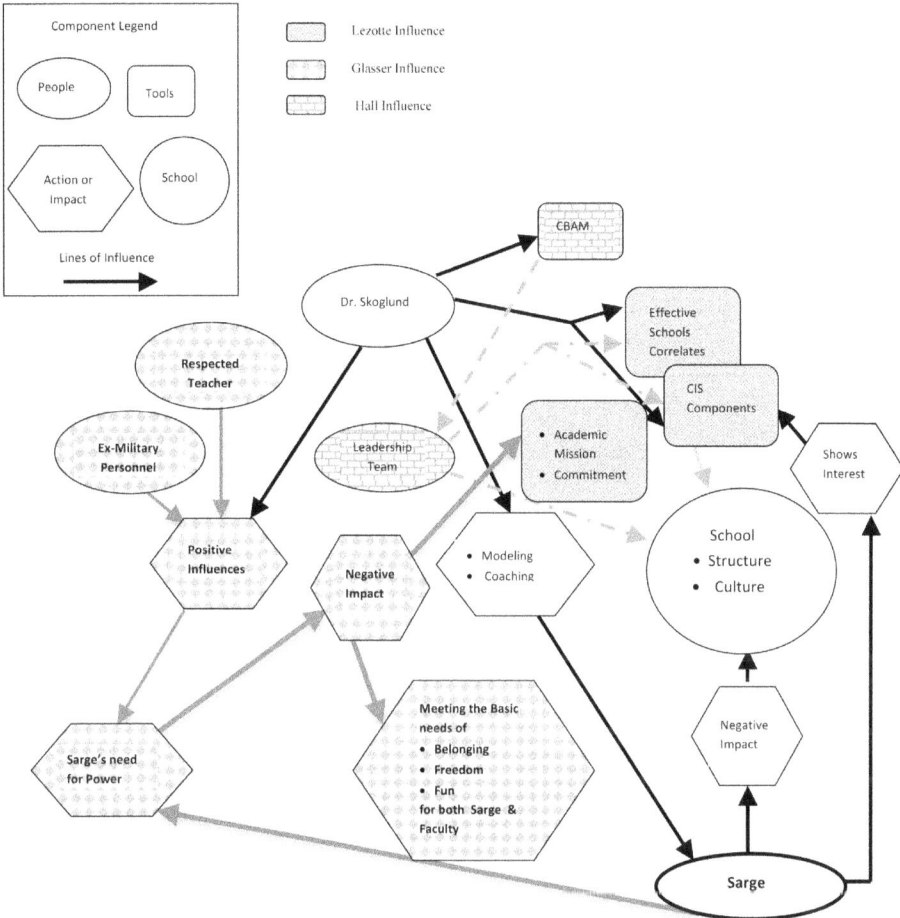

Figure 3.1.

SUMMARY

- People naturally experience concerns when they face a change.
- These concerns can be identified and interventions can be employed.
- The person's concern must be addressed before he or she will fully accept the change.
- Applying an inappropriate intervention will not address the person's concern. An inappropriate response will usually intensify the concern.
- CBAM techniques are an effective tool to identify the conditions that are preventing the successful implementation of an innovation.

- Just listening to people's concerns has a positive impact on their need to belong.

YOUR TASK

During our conversation, Sarge clearly demonstrated the stage of concern that he was experiencing. Identify the stage and develop a plan for how you would assist Sarge through that stage.

_____
_____
_____
_____

4

Get With It!

Dr. Frederick Herzberg, The Motivation to Work

Photo 4.1. Dr. Frederick Herzberg.

Sarge was now having his needs for belonging, fun, and freedom met, at least to some degree. His social group had become a source of real enjoyment for him. He felt accepted by friends and was gaining respect from the faculty. The superintendent was no longer constantly looking over his shoulder. His need for power was diminishing, but he still reverted to his military persona at times and issued orders. This, in fact, was appropriate in certain situations. The difference was that he now recognized what he was doing and was making conscious decisions about his behavior.

Given these new conditions, I began to look for ways to keep Mr. Wilson progressing and give him tools to bring out the highest possible level of performance from the faculty. The research on motivation in the workplace done by Dr. Frederick Herzberg, once again, proved to be a very valuable tool. Motivation has long been a fascinating topic of discussion and research. Both are often complicated by the multiple definitions of motivation that are offered:

- The condition of being eager to do something (*Merriam-Webster's Learner's Dictionary*)
- Any force that causes someone to act (*Merriam-Webster's Learner's Dictionary*)
- The desire to do something (*Oxford Dictionary*)
- The reason one has for acting (Online dictionary)

Dr. Herzberg's interest was centered on how to lead people to consistently give their best effort in the workplace and he saw the definitions above as being so broad as to be unusable for his purpose.

He would consider scenarios such as the following and then ask some insightful questions:

> A manager desires a higher level of performance from an employee and so yells at the person and demands better performance or the person would be fired. Who is motivated—the boss who is yelling or the employee who is embarrassed and threatened by being yelled at? Will the manager's behavior cause the employee to elevate his or her performance over the long term? Will the manager's behavior damage the working relationship with the employee and others who witness the exchange?
>
> Suppose the boss calls a meeting and tells everyone that there has been a big problem on the production line and, as a result, the company could lose the contract with their biggest client. If this happens, several jobs would be lost. This can be avoided if everyone agrees to work two hours overtime each day for a week and complete their tasks faster and without errors. Will most people be good employees and step up in this situation? This may cause people to elevate their performance over the time of the crisis but will it cause them to maintain that level of performance over the long term?

Herzberg viewed motivation as "an internal drive that is activated when a person chooses, of their own free will, to behave in a given manner over the long term."

Consider another scenario. Suppose the boss calls a meeting of all the employees of the company and explains that a new production procedure is going to be implemented and that it will require a certain level of computer skills. The boss displays compassion by stating that he or she understands that this is a surprise and that not everyone may be interested or be able to afford the training required and assures everyone that no jobs would be lost. People who did not possess the skills would be placed in different positions in the company or with a sister company. Under these conditions, it is probable that some people would choose to obtain the training and some would not. The people who freely chose to obtain the training were *motivated* by their own desire to upgrade their skills. They were not forced to do so.

Dr. Herzberg's research was conducted in multiple types of organizations and in multiple locations. The result of the research was the identification of two categories of factors present in the workplace. One category of factors produced job satisfaction and, thus, caused workers to choose to maintain a high level of performance or to elevate their level of performance over the long term. The second category of factors produced sources of dissatisfaction in the workplace. These conditions tend to diminish people's performance.

Herzberg determined that the following factors found in the workplace tended to produce *job satisfaction* and so were considered "motivational" factors:

- ACHIEVEMENT: This is defined as the internal sense of satisfaction gained by seeing the results of one's work. The feeling a person experiences when the person successfully completes a task or finds a solution to a problem.
- RECOGNITION: This factor is produced by praise from a supervisor or peer. It may take such forms as a letter of commendation, a compliment in front of peers, a raise, a promotion, or a private conversation during which respect is demonstrated for the person and/or the work accomplished by the person.
- THE WORK ITSELF: This factor exists when the person simply enjoys the work he or she is doing. The work is gratifying and holds the person's interest. It contributes to the person's sense of self-worth.
- RESPONSIBILITY: This results from being trusted to make decisions, work unsupervised, and to supervise the work of others.
- ADVANCEMENT: This is the sense of satisfaction a person experiences from being promoted to a higher-level position and/or given greater responsibility.
- GROWTH: This factor is produced by the opportunity to attain new knowledge and new or advanced skills.

It is important to note that these factors are found in the content of the work itself as opposed to the working environment.

The following factors are found in the work environment and tend to produce *job dissatisfaction*:

- COMPANY POLICY AND ADMINISTRATION: This factor is the result of a belief that the organization is poorly structured to accomplish its goals and the organization's policies are harmful personally

(poor wages) or professionally (promotions are impacted by discrimination).
- SUPERVISION AND SUPERVISOR RELATIONS: This is the result of a feeling that the supervisor is lacking knowledge and incompetent to perform the job and is also unfair in administering policy.
- WORKING CONDITIONS: People feel dissatisfaction when the condition of the workplace is below standards, tools and materials required to successfully complete the work are lacking, and the amount of work demanded is unreasonable.
- SALARY: This is a concern that the wage being paid is unfair compensation.

These factors diminish people's satisfaction on the job and tend to lower the level of job performance.

Figure 4.1 depicts the impact of these factors and their relative power to influence people's performance.

It should be noted that the bars representing each of the factors extend into both the satisfaction and dissatisfaction fields. This occurred for a variety of reasons. First, it represents individual preferences. Using recognition as an example, one person might be very pleased to receive public recognition from a supervisor. A second person might be shy and wish to avoid the attention.

To state the obvious, leaders of organizations must focus on introducing and maintaining job satisfaction factors in the workplace while reducing, or even better, eliminating the job dissatisfaction factors. Conducting individual and/or group conferences using Concerns-Based Adoption Model techniques will usually lead to insights that will assist the leaders to accomplish this goal.

Herzberg acknowledged that people could be forced into a short-term behavior by a threat to their well-being. He also noted that people will elevate their performance during a crisis but return to their typical level when the crisis had passed. This was not what was desired in the workplace. He urged leaders of organizations to accept that motivation is an internal drive that is activated when one chooses, of one's own free will, to behave in a given manner over the long term. Given that, leaders must then accept that they cannot "inject" motivation into anyone. The goal must be to create an environment in which people will, of their own free will, choose to elevate their performance over the long term.

Dr. Herzberg defined a set of practices designed to impact factors that produced job satisfaction. He called this concept *vertical job loading*. The idea of vertical is critical to the process. Asking someone to do something that is new, different, and challenging was considered a reward and these things tended to activate the person's internal drive (motivation) to gain

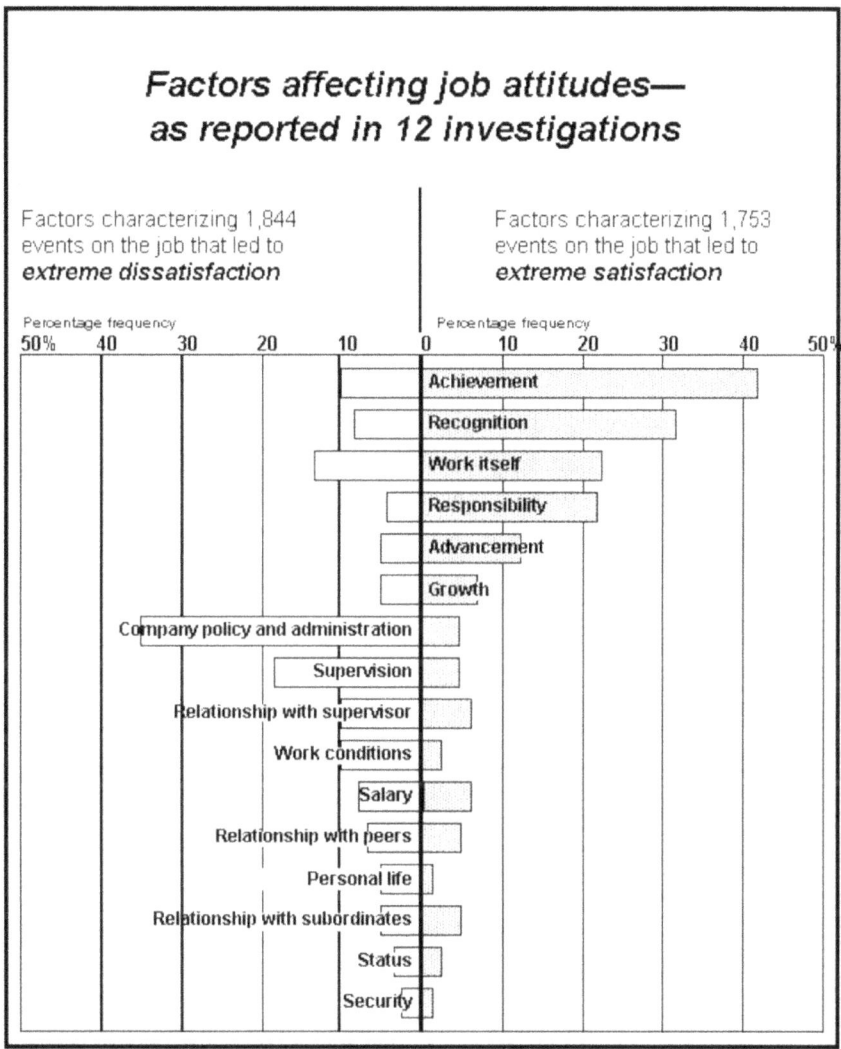

Figure 4.1.

knowledge and perform at a higher level. Asking someone to take on more of the same, identified as horizontal job loading, was often considered punishment for doing something well and produced job dissatisfaction.

Vertical job loading involves such practices as the following:

- REMOVE CONTROLS: This involves, when appropriate, giving the person the freedom and authority to accomplish the person's task as he or she so desires.

- **INCREASE ACCOUNTABILITY:** Acknowledge that with freedom and authority comes responsibility. People feel good about being given additional freedom and authority and tend to raise their level of performance when they know they will be held accountable.
- **MAKE AN EXPERT:** Create the opportunity for a person to become an expert in a field of interest and celebrate that person's knowledge and skill.
- **GRANT AUTHORITY:** Show respect for the person by assigning new and more challenging tasks and indicating confidence in his or her ability to do the job.
- **REPORT TO PEERS:** Build esteem for the person with colleagues by having the person share new knowledge and demonstrate high-quality work.

One of the keys to creating motivational conditions for people is to find a person's passion and then remove roadblocks as the person pursues his or her passion.

Table 4.1. Vertical Job Loading

Principle	What To Do	Factor Impacted
Remove Controls (when and where appropriate)	• Remove a current restriction	Achievement
	• Allow to work with minimal supervision	
	• Assign a task and allow person to determine the process	Responsibility
Grant Authority	• Allow person to make appropriate decisions	Achievement
	• Assign person to supervise others	Recognition
	• Assign person to develop a process or product	Responsibility
Increase Accountability	• Tell person "I trust you to do this" (privately and in front of others)	Recognition
	• Require person to demonstrate accomplishment of self/others	Responsibility
	• Send someone to person for advice	
Make an Expert	• Identify area of interest and tell person "I need you to be the expert"	Advancement
	• Send person to a seminar, class, etc.	Growth
	• Provide study materials	Recognition
	• Assign person to train others	Responsibility
Report to Peers	• Report on a conference or successful project	Recognition
	• Present a new concept/program	Responsibility

Table 4.1 gives directions as to what to do when employing vertical job loading principles and which of the job satisfaction factors are affected by the action.

It should be noted that while a sense of achievement is the most powerful factor in producing job satisfaction, responsibility is impacted by each vertical job loading principle. People tend to "step up" when they feel that they are trusted to perform a task and respected for their work.

I was very pleased with the progress Sarge was making and wanted to move him and the leadership team to a higher level of performance. I decided to use CBAM techniques, job satisfaction factors, and vertical job loading principles to do this.

SARGE'S STORY

Dr. S.: We have now completed one semester of implementing the CIS. When you assess what is happening in your school, what are your immediate concerns?

Sarge: I feel much more confident in using the system, but each time we tour the school or meet with the leadership team, you come up with some detail that makes us more effective. I want to know all that you know so I can answer the questions that the teachers ask and not depend on you.

Dr. S.: Understanding all the nuances of the system is simply a function of time and experience. You are progressing faster than I anticipated and I'm very pleased by your work with the CIS. You should be proud of what you have done.

Sarge: Thanks, I just still feel like there is so much more to learn.

Dr. S.: Tell me how you feel about the leadership team and the work they are doing.

Sarge: They are still learning too, but they seem much more comfortable working together. As I sit in on their meetings, I hear them willingly sharing ideas and I'll bet you see the same when you conduct their meetings. They are asking to visit the school that you took me to when we started this. Do you think that is a good idea?

Dr. S.: Yes, that's a great idea. If you can arrange coverage for the team for a day, I'll make the arrangements with the principal for the visit.

Sarge: There is something that is coming up that I am very concerned about. Later in this semester, I will have to build the master class schedule for next year and I have no idea how to do that!

Dr. S.: I'm aware of a conference on that skill that has been attended by several other principals with whom I've worked. They came away feeling like they were now experts in schedule construction. Would you like me to make arrangements with the superintendent for you to attend?

Sarge: Yes, learning how to do that would be a great relief. There is something else that I need help with. Teachers keep asking me questions about constructing formative assessments that are valid and reliable. I don't know what those terms mean!

Dr. S.: Those are very important issues and it is to your benefit to learn as much as you can about assessments and accountability. I would suggest a university class and frequent dialogue with your district director of assessment. I also want to give the people on the leadership team more responsibility. They need to be conducting their own meetings. Let's make some plans to prepare them to do that.

During our conversation, I was very pleased to hear that both Sarge and the leadership team members were continuing to experience information concerns. The fact that they were willing to admit that they did not yet know all they needed to know and wanted to learn more was very encouraging.

I made a couple of decisions as the conversation progressed. The first was to use the job satisfaction factor of recognition with Sarge. The second was to use the vertical job loading factor of making him an expert. Building a school's master class schedule is a complicated task. When it is done poorly, it can quickly activate the job dissatisfaction factors associated with company policy, supervisor relations, and working conditions. I did not want to take the chance of introducing those factors when there was a way to teach Sarge the skills that would avoid them.

From the beginning of the school year, either Sarge or I attended each instructional team meeting and usually conducted the meeting. Our purpose was to ensure that the team leaders had role models and every team member was made aware of how the meeting should be conducted and what the outcome should be. Following a couple of review meetings with the team leaders, I was confident that they would have the skills they needed to effectively conduct the meetings. It was now time to give them more responsibility and let them know that they were now accountable for the work accomplished by their teams. For the next couple of weeks, Sarge and I simply observed but did not participate in the meetings. Following the meetings, we would provide feedback to the team leaders and soon the meetings were running smoothly. We publicly thanked the leaders for their desire to learn and for the effectiveness of the work they were now doing. We also announced Sarge's enrollment in the schedule-building conference. In order to make this important to the faculty, we asked for a written response to the CBAM question, "When I think of my schedule for next year, I'm concerned about . . ."

This proved to be a valuable piece of information for Sarge as he participated in the training.

We made arrangements to spend a full day visiting the school that was successfully using the CIS. Each member of our visiting team was assigned to shadow their counterpart during the day. The day ended with a debriefing meeting where both teams shared their experiences and helpful thoughts. The meeting ended with sincere best wishes and the commitment to continue the communication and collaboration. The leadership team talked excitedly on the bus ride home about all they had learned and how they were immediately going to employ what they had

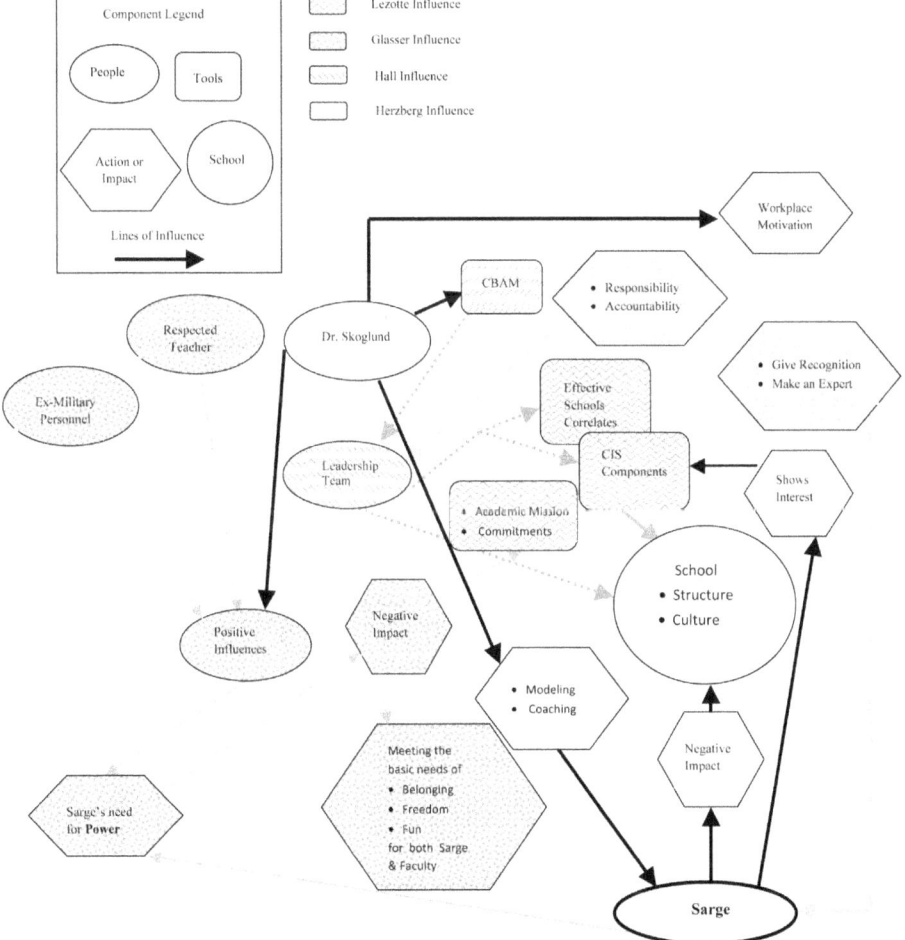

Figure 4.2.

learned. As the day ended, each member of the leadership team expressed gratitude for the experience. Over the next couple of weeks, what they had learned became visible in the workings of the school. Sarge and the principal of the other school had frequent phone conversations and both were pleased with their ability to collaborate and offer support to each other when the inevitable issues surfaced.

As I planned to use Dr. Herzberg's work, I added the ideas to the mind map. Being able to see the visual image was very helpful as I determined which of the job factors and which of the vertical job loading principles to use and with whom to use them.

The newest phase of the map shows how I planned to use the vertical job loading principles of responsibility and accountability to influence the performance of the leadership team. The job satisfaction factor of recognition and the vertical job loading principle of becoming an expert were used to create an environment in which Sarge could choose to elevate his performance.

SUMMARY

- Motivation is an internal drive and so, by definition, it must be activated by the individual. It cannot be injected by an external force.
- People will change their short-term behavior in response to personal threat or a crisis in the workplace.
- Long-term behavior change occurs when an environment is created where the person freely chooses to change a behavior.
- Remember that "behavior is a matter of choice" and so a person can choose to (1) maintain a current behavior, (2) adopt a new behavior, or (3) replace an unsuccessful behavior with a new behavior that would produce the desired result.
- Vertical job loading principles are powerful tools when used with integrity. If people sense that they are simply being manipulated, their performance typically declines.
- Rewards (false motivators), like paying a child for every A on the report card, are enticing because they sometimes do work in the short term. The danger lies in two areas: (1) the goal for the child now becomes the money and not the learning and (2) when the money stops there is a high probability that the desire to learn will be negatively impacted. Teaching the child the joy of achievement—learning for the sake of learning—is the key to a long-term desire to learn. Dr. Alfie Kohn carefully explains this phenomenon in *Punished by Rewards*.

YOUR TASK

Review the job satisfaction factors and determine which of these you see as potentially having the greatest impact if it were to be become part of the environment in Mr. Wilson's school. When you have made your selection, develop a plan to put this factor in place. Remember, this is a change so pay attention to the stage(s) of concern these people will most likely experience and have intervention prepared.

_____
_____
_____
_____

5

✢

The System Did It!

Dr. Peter Senge, The Fifth Discipline: The Art & Practice of the Learning Organization and Schools That Learn

Photo 5.1. Dr. Peter Senge. Printed by permission of Dr. Peter Senge.

Dr. Peter Senge's work on systems is, at once, extremely complicated and wonderfully simple. You may have to read a passage more than once to fully understand it but you will come to a place where you will say to yourself, "Yes, I get it. Of course that is right."

Dr. Senge teaches us all about systems, what they are, how they function, how we function within them, and why it is so critical that we recognize their presence and acknowledge their power. To emphasize the point, please consider the following:

Name something that has no impact on anything else and nothing else has an impact on it.

Don't spend a lot of time thinking of an answer. No such thing exists. We tend to think in linear terms; however, the world consists of a never-ending milieu of interrelated systems. Think of planting seeds that interact with the dirt (soil system); the seeds are nurtured by the sun and the rain (weather system). The seeds eventually grow into a tree that produces the oxygen we need to breathe and survive through the photosynthesis process (ecosystem). The fruit from the tree becomes part of our food chain and nourishes the very complex systems that are our bodies.

Nothing stands alone.

So, what is a system? *Webster* defines a system as "a combination of things forming a complex or unitary whole."

Our tendency to think in linear terms often leads us into making errors because we miss the big picture. Making a change in one part of a production line in hopes of improving productivity must be done with consideration to the impact the change in this single station has on the other stations in the line. Changing one cog in a fine timepiece without making adjustments to the other cogs in the system can only lead to disaster.

If we apply the system concept to human interaction, a very interesting phenomenon may occur.

Have you ever been involved with a group of people that just "clicked"? If so, I'm confident that you remember it as an uplifting experience. It may have been a sports team, a church choir, a book club, a group of colleagues at work, a college study group, or any one of many other groups.

If you have enjoyed this rare experience, Dr. Senge would surmise that the people in your group were:

- People that you liked personally and respected professionally,
- People who shared a passion for the activity and were committed to continually improving their knowledge and skills,
- People who trusted each other enough to put forth ideas with no fear of ridicule,
- People who carried their share of the load and willingly picked up an extra load for a colleague who was unable to perform for a short time, or
- People who understood the environment (system) in which they functioned and how they could influence it.

It is almost certain that the group did not start out this way—this relationship didn't happen by chance. The group learned to behave in this way. The interaction among the members of the group as they learned to become a cohesive and productive unit is another example of a system.

Dr. Senge declares that successful organizations of the future will have teams such as this functioning at every level of the organization. The modern world has become a very complex place—a place where traditional top-down management has outlived its usefulness. In order to be truly effective in the future, organizations must learn how to gain commitment from people at all levels of the organization and create an environment where all people continually demonstrate a desire to learn and to perform at the highest level.

In his bestselling book *The Fifth Discipline*, Senge carefully explained how an organization can learn to create this very special environment by committing to the practice of five fields of learning (disciplines). The disciplines are: shared vision, personal mastery, mental models, team learning, and systems thinking. Senge intentionally identified the fifth discipline as "systems thinking" because it is the discipline that brings everything together. In simple terms, this is the ability to see and understand the interconnectedness of all the parts of a whole.

In a follow-up book, *Schools That Learn*, he demonstrated how these disciplines can be applied in an educational setting. As you read about these disciplines, think about how they can be introduced and practiced in your organization.

THE DISCIPLINES

These disciplines are not reforms or programs to be implemented. They are ongoing fields of study that perpetuate the search for new knowledge and skill. When this quest is pursued by individuals and groups within an organization, the organization becomes a learning organization.

Shared Vision

The Effective Schools Correlate of clear and focused mission is a similar concept with the exception that a clear and focused mission can be defined and imposed upon a school by a strong principal.

A shared vision cannot be imposed. It may be inspired by a single person, but it is much more than a single person imposing his or her will on an organization. Even if you and I have a common understanding of what our organization is attempting to accomplish, it is still not enough. We must be committed to each other in our passion for the vision and in our attempt to achieve the vision.

Recall a bit of history. What is the quote that most people recall from President Kennedy's inaugural speech? Did the words "Ask not what your country can do for you. Ask what you can do for your country" come to mind? This was a wonderful sound bite and it played well in the news media. However, it did little to change the country. JFK did say something in his speech that not only changed the country, it changed the world! He stated that we would put a man on the moon and return him safely to Earth. This single statement absolutely drove NASA during the mid-to-late 60s. There were no speeches by NASA administrators or fancy documents displayed in the NASA labs, but everyone at NASA was driven by a passion to accomplish the mission. This is the power of a shared vision.

The NASA experience clearly demonstrates the difference between compliance and commitment. Millions of people go to work every day and comply with the requirements of their job. People will comply for many reasons. They may see themselves a team players, they may be seeking a promotion, or they may simply fear the loss of their jobs. None of these reasons produce a commitment to a vision. People who are committed to a vision pursue the vision for its own sake. They believe in the vision. People who are committed to a vision pursue the vision with great enthusiasm and, at times, sacrifice.

You would find a shared vision at work in the group described in the beginning of this chapter. A shared vision binds people together and creates an intensity of focus. It is a source of excitement that has the power to uplift people's aspirations. It is what changes "the" organization to "our" organization.

A vision is spread across an organization through an ongoing dialogue. The vision is a constant topic of conversation both as an item on meeting agendas (formal) and in lunchroom conversation (informal). The limitations to this often occur in the form of time and workload demands. These immediate demands may blur the vision of the future. "I can't be bothered with that now, just leave me alone and let me do my job." It is the responsibility of the leadership of the organization to keep the vision alive, vibrant, and at the forefront of people's thoughts.

Figure 5.1 is a visual representation of this pattern. The loop on the left demonstrates how a vision is spread across an organization. The competing loop on the right demonstrates the factors that inhibit the spread of the vision.

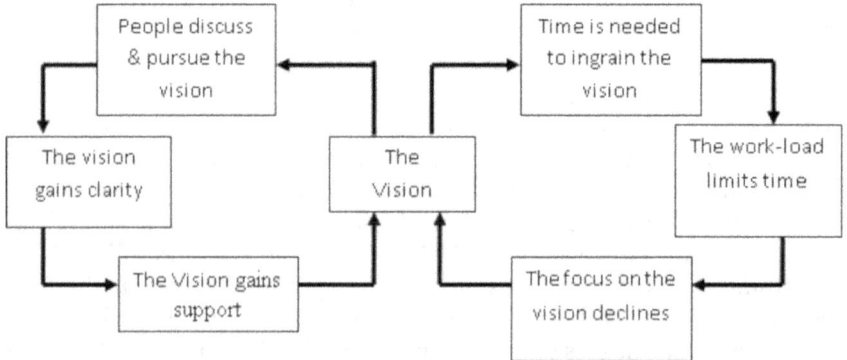

Figure 5.1.

Effective leaders are able to assist people through the changes that are an integral part of committing to a vision. Leaders must take care not to allow the focus on the daily demands of accomplishing the work to take away from the focus on the vision itself.

Individuals cannot be forced to commit to a shared vision; they must come to accept a shared vision through joint inquiry and dialogue. A vision will become a viable force only when people believe they have control over their environment and can shape their own future. The Concerns-Based Adoption Model can be an effective tool as leaders seek to create a shared vision.

Shared Vision in the School

Creating an environment where a shared vision can form and flourish is initiated through the identification of the academic mission and the core commitments and formalized in the writing of a school vision statement. The faculty must be directly and intensely involved in the creation of all these documents. These documents must be the topic of ongoing dialogues conducted in faculty meetings and instructional team meetings. It is critical to the success of the CIS that the faculty feels a real ownership in and commitment to the messages set forth in these documents.

Shared Vision in the Classroom

The teacher, on the first day of school, should explain the school's academic mission to the students and how it is depicted on the classroom data chart. The students in the class should then enter into a dialogue exploring the level that has been set by the faculty and whether the class wants to set a higher level for the classroom. The class should also identify a set of core commitments for the classroom. A dialogue should then be conducted throughout the year concerning how the class is performing as measured against the academic mission and the core commitments that have been identified by the class.

Remember, this is a journey—not an event!

Personal Mastery

The concept embodied in the discipline of personal mastery was at the very core of the US Army slogan "Be all that you can be!"

Personal mastery is the discipline of the lifelong pursuit of personal growth. It has its origin in an individual's personal vision. It requires a person to accurately assess and accept the current level of performance and then demonstrate a willingness to seek the growth necessary to effectively achieve a personal vision. It is this commitment to continuous personal growth by individuals that is the spiritual core of a learning organization. A learning organization is one that continually seeks to understand the present and expand its capacity to create its future. Such an organization learns to understand the complexities of the world and adapt.

In order to demonstrate the two components of personal mastery, let us consider the weekend golfer (Joe). Joe must first accept that he is a twenty handicapper and the weakest part of his game is putting. If he is satisfied with being a twenty handicapper or if he sees himself as having a two handicap, he will have no reason to pursue growth. If his personal vision is to be the best golfer he can be, he must then make the commitment to take lessons and spend the hours at the driving range and on the putting green that are necessary to improve his skills.

When we are driven by personal mastery, we must accept that we will never completely achieve the vision. There will always be a gap between a personal vision and the current level of performance. This gap, called creative tension, is a powerful source of positive energy. When we recognize the presence of creative tension, we must also accept that there are only two possible ways to relieve the tension: (1) pull the current level of performance up toward the vision—experience growth or (2) pull the vision down toward the current level of performance—lower the goal. The unintended consequence of lowering the goal is that it becomes addictive. Each time we feel the tension, we can easily relieve it by lowering the goal.

Lowering the goal is easy! It requires no effort! It is, however, only a response to a symptom. We will always be better served by employing a systemic (system-wide) solution, such as improving the skill level that is necessary to close the gap between our current level of performance and our personal vision. If we choose not to respond to this creative tension in a systemic manner, what we lose is the vision and the commitment that it created.

Apply this thought to the current standards and testing environment that is now so prevalent in American education. There is tremendous pressure on schools to raise the test scores above the current level of performance. This activates creative tension. The diagram on the following page demonstrates how the two approaches to relieving the creative tension interact. By inserting the arrows, the ebb and flow of the creative tension becomes visible.

Pressure to raise academic achievement is the presenting symptom and loop 1 demonstrates lowering the expectations as a response to increased pressure. As the pressure to raise student achievement goes up, the pressure can be relieved by moving the expectations down. This is the easy way out, but it will never generate a long-term solution to raising student achievement. The danger in following this loop is that it is addictive and

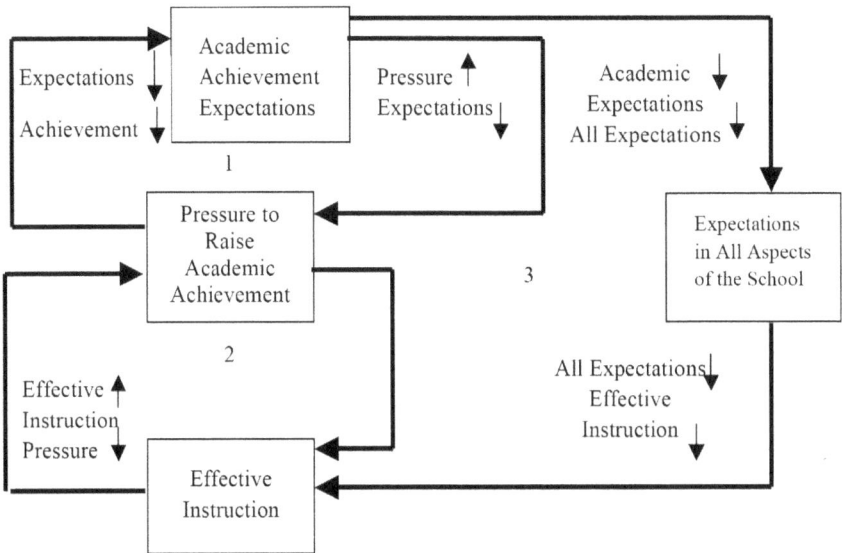

Figure 5.2.

activates the unintended consequences seen in loop 3. Lowering the expectations for academic performance can become generalized and, thus, a response to not only the academic achievement situation but to many other aspects of the school. Lower academic expectations typically lead to less effective instruction. When loop 3 is active, it makes implementing the long-term solution depicted in loop 2 much more difficult because the pressure in loop 2 is relieved by more effective instruction and loop 3 has caused less effective instruction.

Honestly facing our current level of performance and seeking personal growth means taking risks. People are more likely to attempt to make personal changes in an environment where they feel safe to challenge the status quo and explore new methods (remember the personal concern stage in the CBAM model).

Personal mastery flows from an individual's personal vision. This vision is fueled by the internal drive called motivation. Dr. Dan Lortie discusses an educator's internal or intrinsic rewards in his book *Schoolteacher*. Lortie states, "Teachers experienced the greatest satisfaction from knowing that they had reached their students and the students had learned." While educators who seek personal mastery often enjoy this thrill, it is a satisfaction that eludes those who accept poor performance by students and by themselves.

If we are to assist people in their pursuit of personal mastery, we must understand what factors move individuals to elevate the level of performance (remember Herzberg's job satisfaction factors and vertical job loading).

> The core of leadership strategy is simple: be a model. Commit yourself to your own personal mastery. Talking about personal mastery may open people's minds somewhat, but actions always speak louder than words. There's nothing more powerful you can do to encourage others in their quest for personal mastery than to be serious in your own quest.
>
> —Dr. Peter Senge

Personal Mastery in the School

In the Continuous Improvement System, classroom data charts and grade-level (subject) data charts are a vivid real-time depiction of the current level of student achievement. The data may cause a teacher to consider the effectiveness of instruction being offered to students and this may be the origin of personal growth as the teacher seeks to acquire new instructional skills. This may also occur as a group if the teachers discover that students across a grade level are struggling with a specific concept.

Personal Mastery in the Classroom

The Continuous Improvement System requires each student to maintain a data chart that tracks his or her personal progress. This is a powerful tool for the teacher to use to open a dialogue with the student and assist the student to set personal goals that elevate his or her level of achievement.

Mental Models

This is the discipline of self-reflection. It is focused on identifying and understanding our own personal attitudes, biases, and perceptions as well as those held by the people with whom we interact. Dr. Senge describes mental models as the filtering lenses through which we view our world. They consist of all the beliefs, assumptions, generalizations, and biases that the accumulation of our life's experiences has led us to adopt. Because no two individuals have had exactly the same experiences, mental models are unique to each individual. Our mental models impact every aspect of our lives. They influence how we view ourselves, our personal relationships, the performance of others, and our own performance at work and even how we interpret a piece of art.

A mental model may be expressed in a simple generalization—boys are better at math than girls. A mental model may be expressed as something very complex. Because people hold mental models unique to themselves, people with differing mental models may view the same occurrence and draw very different conclusions. Child A and Child B engage in a playground fight. Two other children (C and D) observe the fight. Child C might report that Child B started the fight while Child D might report exactly the opposite. Even though they observed exactly the same event, the mental models they hold led them to different interpretations of the event.

Understanding mental models is critical to efficient and effective communication. Suppose you are an elementary school principal about to meet with the father of a child who is struggling and you know that the father will want to visit the classroom. The father is a firefighter who has spoken on fire safety at your school several times. If you entered the classroom and the father observed every wall covered with children's papers, you could anticipate that his focus might shift to the fire danger the papers present and away from his daughter's academic struggles. By understanding his mental model, you could ask the teacher to remove the papers prior to your visit and thus maintain the focus on developing a plan to assist the daughter.

Understanding another person's mental model(s) is important; however, it is equally important to understand our own. The most dangerous mental models are the ones we do not know we hold or deny that we hold.

I spent many years in a district-level administrative position that required me to supervise all the junior high schools and high schools in a large metropolitan school district. I was very aware that I held a negative mental model regarding a popular activity that was conducted in each of the schools. Because I recognized this, whenever an issue concerning this activity arose, I always involved a second person to ensure that my negative mental model did not influence the outcome of the issue.

The failure to understand mental models is dangerous because they always present us with an incomplete/inaccurate picture. This makes the use of data critical! Without data, we are prone to make giant leaps from abstractions to generalizations. This is known as climbing the ladder of inference. Consider the following example based on an actual occurrence.

A high school drama department had rehearsed for weeks to present the musical *Camelot*. A week before opening night, a teacher from the school was getting her hair done and overheard a conversation between the client and hairdresser at the next station. The client was expressing her displeasure that a high school would present a production that so heavily emphasizes an extramarital affair. She stated that she felt she must gather her church group and do something about this.

The teacher returned to school and reported this to the drama teacher, who immediately warned the principal that the musical would be protested and opening night would probably be picketed. Plans were made to deal with the anticipated protest. Of course, opening night was a great success. No protesters were ever seen and the local paper gave student performances rave reviews.

The teacher took in a small piece of data (the conversation she overheard), made some assumptions based on her mental models (religious hard-liners following through on a threat), drew a faulty conclusion (the performance will surely be protested), and took the inappropriate action of sounding a premature alarm. This climb up the ladder of inference led to a great deal of the wasted time and effort preparing for a conflict that never developed. This happened because the conclusion was not based on factual data.

Mental models influence everything from interaction between neighbors to interaction on a global scale. The diagram below demonstrates how mental models and climbing the ladder of inference can quickly escalate a minor occurrence into a major conflict.

Begin in the center and follow the arrows. The loop on the left shows how A perceives an action taken by B as a threat and takes some action in response. The loop on the right shows how B sees the responsive action by A as a threat and takes additional action, which A sees as a greater threat and so A takes another responsive action. As the cycle repeats, the actions taken by both A and B become more extreme.

This is what causes a person to look across the yard at a neighbor's new car and then go out and buy a bigger and more expensive car—the "keeping up with the Joneses" syndrome. It is what happens when a student acts out in a classroom and the teacher responds in a way that backs the student into a corner and leaves him or her no option but to come out fighting. It is what causes price wars between service stations located on opposite corners of an intersection. It is what fueled the Cold War between the United States and the USSR. The USSR saw the nuclear

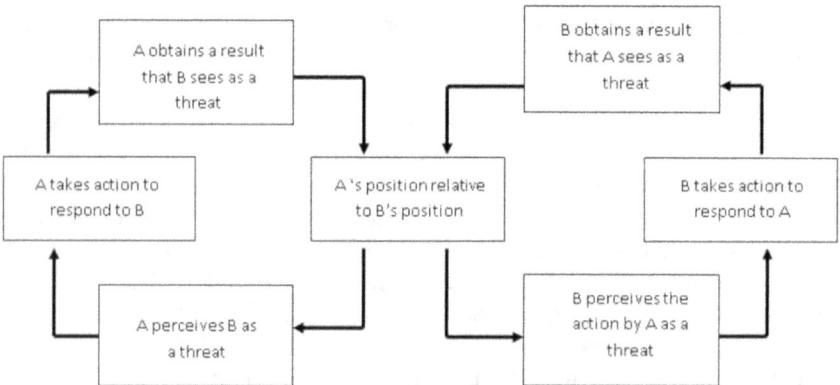

Figure 5.3.

arsenal assembled by the United States and responded by building more of its own. This went on until the Cuban Missile Crisis. If the leaders of the USSR had not backed down, the world could have been plunged into nuclear devastation.

These examples point out the critical need for people to understand the roles of dialogue and advocacy as they meet to address complicated problems. Each person will enter the meeting with his or her own mental model in place; each person will typically come prepared to advocate for his or her position. Effective teams will be able to put all the proposed options created by differing mental models before the group to be fully examined without fear of recrimination. This process involves only dialogue where ideas are exchanged, explored, and enhanced. Advocacy should enter only when the options have been fully explored and narrowed to the point where two or three of the best options have been identified. This is the time for individuals to advocate for one option and provide a rationale for doing so. This is the time for a vote to be taken and a decision to be made.

If the dialogue portion of the meeting is forgone, each person will advocate for his or her own position, and the problem-solving aspect of the meeting is lost as advocacy begets advocacy. This behavior is what has precipitated the gridlock that has often occurred in the U.S. Congress as our elected politicians adhere to party lines and refuse to seek common ground.

Several years ago, the Hanover Insurance Company was facing severe financial difficulty and adopted a systems-thinking approach to turn the company around. An excerpt from the credo adopted during their reformation seems to be appropriate to conclude this section.

- The effectiveness of the leader is related to the continual examination and clarification of his/her mental models
- A favored mental model should never be imposed on people. Mental models should lead to dialogue and a self-concluding decision
- Self-concluding decisions lead to deeper convictions and more effective implementation
- Multiple mental models bring multiple perspectives to the table and ultimately better decisions

A critical question to be pondered is, "Will we allow our mental models to impede our learning and progress toward our shared vision or will we use them to accelerate the process?"

Mental Models in the School

Mental models in schools are often hidden. This is partially due to the isolation in which teachers typically work. There is little or no opportunity for teachers to engage in professional dialogue and so there is little or no attempt to evaluate and understand the effectiveness of the instructional program or the level of student achievement. The Continuous Improvement System requires teachers to work in instructional teams. These teams must learn the skills required to conduct productive dialogue. The teachers must learn to trust each other to speak freely without fear of recrimination. This takes time and coaching. It is only through dialogue that both individual and collective instruction will become more effective.

Mental Models in the Classroom

Mental Models is a powerful but potentially dangerous discipline to introduce into the classroom. Young children tend to speak their mind quite freely but often without regard to the feelings of others. However, a dialogue with the class concerning respect and how they can work together to attain the academic mission can produce very positive results.

Team Learning

Team learning is the phenomenon that raises the collective IQ of a group significantly above the IQ of any individual member of the group. It builds on the disciplines of shared vision and mental models. Groups that practice this discipline have learned to effectively pursue personal mastery.

Noted contemporary physicist and quantum theorist Dr. David Bohm thoughtfully explores the art of dialogue in his book *On Dialogue*. Bohm stressed that dialogue is not an activity to be won. The goal of dialogue is to completely explore a topic. In this process, the exploration must not stop when the first workable solution is identified. Exploration must go on until the best solution is identified.

Team learning is a skill that must be learned and refined. To be effective in the future, leaders will need to foster a learning environment and move past the mental model that the leader must know all the answers. Hanging on to this mental model will inhibit the growth of the organization the leader is purporting to build.

Bohm identified three conditions that must be present if a group is to engage in the free flow of ideas through a true dialogue.

All participants must "suspend" their assumptions. This must occur in two ways. First, the individual must recognize assumptions as assumptions and not facts. These must be set aside and not allowed to interfere with the free exchange of ideas. Second, the individual must be willing to "suspend"—hold out in full view of others—assumptions for the purpose of being examined.

Finally, all participants must regard each other as colleagues with no power structure involved. A single person should act as a facilitator (not the boss) with the responsibilities of keeping the dialogue on point and denying advocacy until it is appropriate to the process.

Bohm contends that a group engaging in true dialogue will access a larger pool of knowledge that cannot be accessed by individuals in the group who are working alone.

The Continuous Improvement System requires teachers to work in instructional teams. The primary reason for this requirement is to create the conditions under which true dialogue and team learning can occur.

The impact of the dialogue activity involved in team learning can be seen in the diagram below.

This cycle is similar to the one you just saw in the mental models section. Here, however, the outcome is positive. When individuals are willing to learn to work together, good things often happen as a natural result of the dialogue that occurs.

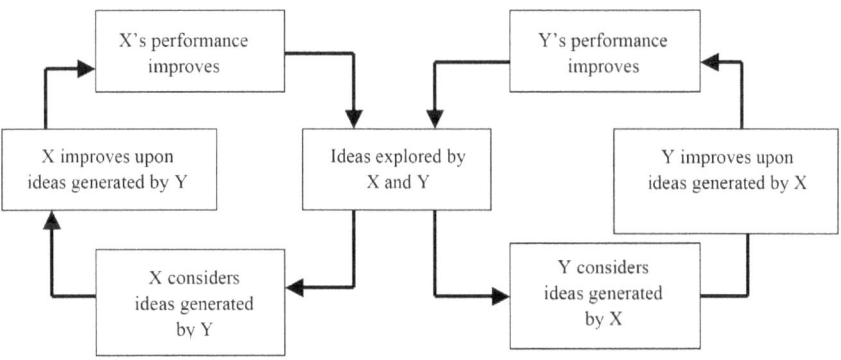

Figure 5.4.

Team Learning in the School

Team learning is at the very heart of the instructional team activities. The agenda for an instructional team meeting always includes items that deal with current levels of student achievement, how instruction on any given objective can be made more effective, and how teachers can collaborate within and across grade levels (subjects) to make instruction more effective. A critical dialogue for teachers is to identify the skills that a student entering a grade level (subject) must have to be successful and to share this with the teachers who are preparing students to advance to that grade level. Those teachers should then have dialogue focused on how to ensure that students are prepared.

Team Learning in the Classroom

When cooperative learning was the hot topic in education, team learning was the foundation of the model. The term "team learning" was never used but the concept was the same. Cooperative learning can be a powerful tool in the classroom if students are properly prepared to participate in the activities.

Systems Thinking

The fifth and final discipline is systems thinking. Systems thinking just might be the most important of the five disciplines.

It is the cornerstone of a learning organization. This discipline brings the first four together. It is a discipline in which we learn to see patterns and the interrelationships of parts as they form a whole. The mind maps that appear near the end of each chapter are visual examples of systems thinking.

Systems thinking is the skill that a principal uses to anticipate the impact of a new communication system. Things such as what happens during the changeover, how long will it take and how will communication be done during that time, what training will people need, how much resistance to the new system can be expected, how will it be overcome, and how long is the learning curve before people can use the new system easily must be considered.

Senge set forth a group of conditions that he labeled *The Laws of the Fifth Discipline*.

Today's problems are often the result of yesterday's solutions. Consider the following scenario: Police have noticed that there has been a significant increase in robberies in the past two weeks. Two weeks ago, police raided a warehouse and confiscated a huge amount of illegal drugs. This reduced the supply on the street, and so the price went up and drug users needed to find ways to secure more cash.

The harder you push, the harder the system pushes back. When someone attempts to implement change in an organization, the most powerful obstacle to overcome is the system that is currently in place. Most people tend to cling to the status quo. Remember the Concerns-Based Adoption Model—you cannot force people through the stages of concern. Pushing harder through an increasingly aggressive intervention, for the most part, is a futile and exhausting effort.

Behavior grows better before it grows worse. Low-level interventions are often alluring because there are times that they actually work—in the short term. Offering a raise in wages for the next month if a large project is completed on time may result in people working harder and completing the project. When the project is complete, workers may bring up, "If there was plenty of money to pay us last month there is probably plenty of money to continue to pay us a better wage. We should hold a work slowdown until we get a permanent raise."

The easy way out usually leads back in. If the wheels on a pair of roller skates are squeaking, squirting water into the bearings will actually stop the annoying noise for a short time. However, the squeaking will eventually return and most likely be accompanied by rust.

The cure really can be worse than the disease. A short-term, non-systemic, cure to a problem can become insidious. A company may decide to increase profit by decreasing personnel costs. This is so easy that the company may become dependent on this as a solution to other problems, such as downsizing to a smaller and less expensive facility. The reduction in personnel can lead to all kinds of issues, such as loss of talent and declining morale. A long-term, systemic cure may have been implemented to increase the quality of the product and a more effective advertising program.

Faster is slower. The optimal growth rate is far less than the maximum growth rate. When growth becomes excessive, the system itself will compensate by losing control of some of the multitude of variables to be managed. Fast growth may lead a company to go into debt buying expensive equipment that later becomes a liability when there is a downturn in business.

Dividing an elephant in half does not produce two small elephants. It is highly probable that, at some point, we have all been told to break a complicated problem into small pieces and solve them one at a time. If we do this, we lose sight of how the whole of the issue functions. We see this concept at work in schools when the charge is to provide a well-rounded education but departments tend to guard their boundaries and deal only with their specific content. The current structure of schools inhibits whole-school team learning and American education would be well served to replace the built-in isolation with collaboration.

Senge stresses that successful organizations in the future will be the ones that are able to see the complexity of the world and learn to adapt to the challenges that this environment presents. The five disciplines he has identified are never mastered. Organizations must constantly work to become more effective in their ongoing pursuit of the disciplines. It is this pursuit that transforms the organization into a learning organization.

Systems thinking helps us to see our world in terms of interrelated wholes and not just disjointed parts. This skill is growing in importance as the world grows more and more complex.

A quote from Peter Senge is a fitting close to this section. He emphasized the fact that dialogue is the key to growth and eloquently expresses

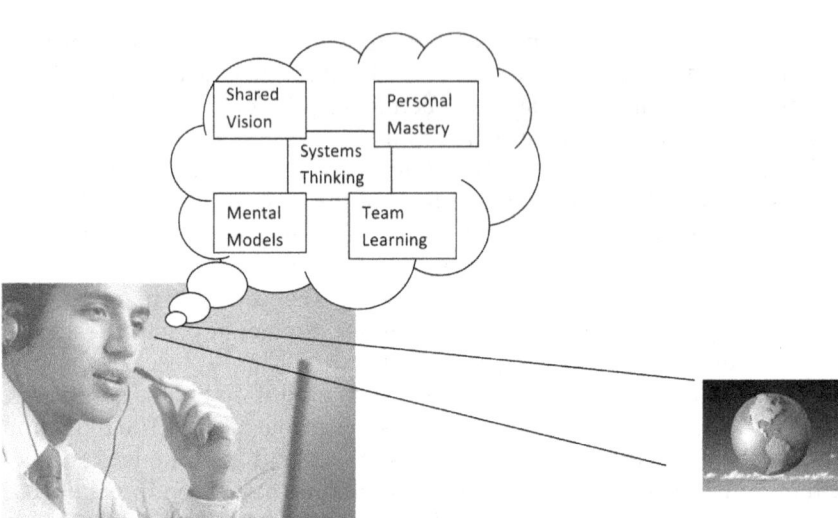

Figure 5.5.

this by saying, "We do not learn nearly as much from discovering an answer as we do from exploring the question."

Systems Thinking in the School

This discipline is critical for the principal and the leadership team as they implement changes in how instruction will be delivered, how student achievement will be measured, and what will be done with the real-time data, along with collaborating with the faculty to determine what professional development activities are desired and will have the greatest impact.

Systems Thinking in the Classroom

This discipline holds great potential for enhancing learning. Teachers must first make students aware of the systemic nature of the world. Think of the impact of an assignment that requires students to explore and explain how a hurricane in the Gulf of Mexico will influence the price of gas in Maine. In science, ask how hydrogen and oxygen form water. The opportunities to engage students in systems thinking are virtually endless.

SYSTEMS THINKING TOOLS

In demonstrating how each of the five disciplines functions, Dr. Senge made extensive use of visual images called archetypes. An archetype is

The System Did It! 61

simply a visual representation of an interactive pattern of events. The basic components of an archetype are reinforcing feedback systems and balancing feedback systems.

Feedback systems and archetypes are very valuable tools if you are seeking to convert a mental image of a complicated issue into a visual image on paper that is much easier to grasp.

Reinforcing Feedback System

Think of this type of system in terms of a vicious (or virtuous) cycle. The mental image of an Olympic downhill skier is appropriate. The skier comes out of the gate at a rather slow speed and then gains speed while progressing down the course. This is a system where each component enhances the next. It is the system of continuing growth or of continuing decline.

Consider this scenario: A charter school has opened in the neighborhood and is seeking to attract new students. The school has quickly acquired a reputation for high levels of academic performance and parent approval. As the satisfied parents communicate with friends, neighbors, and work colleagues, the reputation is spread. This leads to other parents approving of the school and seeking to enroll their students in the school.

A visual representation of this reinforcing feedback system is shown below. Start in the top box and follow the arrows.

Placing arrows beside the components helps to demonstrate how each component impacts the next. In this example, as achievement goes up, parent approval goes up; as approval goes up, the reputation of the school is elevated, and so on. Note how the arrows between each component all point in the same direction. This is characteristic of a reinforcing feedback system. Remember the image of the skier gathering speed as he or she progresses down the course.

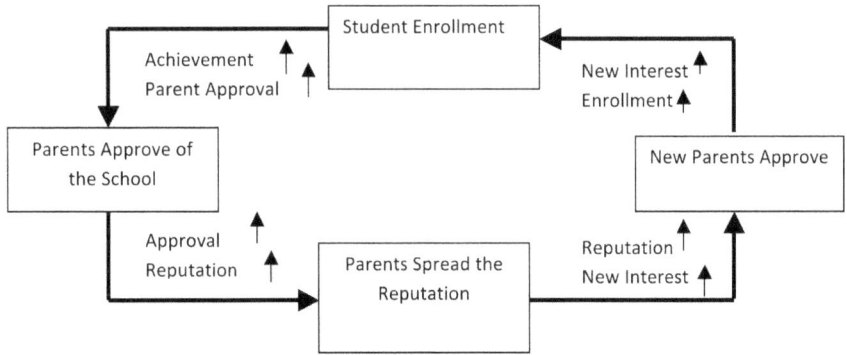

Figure 5.6.

Balancing Feedback System

No cycle of growth or decline runs forever unchecked. At some point, limits are encountered. When limits are introduced into the scenario, a balancing feedback system is formed. In order to grasp a basic concept of a balancing system, you must change your mental image from a downhill skier to the scales of blind justice. A balancing feedback system seeks to obtain equilibrium between components so that as one component goes up the other goes down. Balancing systems tend to maintain the status quo and restrict growth.

To continue the aforementioned scenario, the influx of new students can result in crowded classrooms and difficulty for teachers. This can produce a decline in academic achievement. If the academic achievement level falls, a decline in parent approval will almost certainly follow. Parents again spread the new reputation, which leads to a reduction of new students enrolling and, perhaps, an exodus of current students. Notice that, in a balancing feedback system, some arrows point in opposite directions.

The impact of the balancing feedback system in this scenario is a vivid reminder of why it is so critical to see and understand the big picture of the system with which you are involved. The negative result could have been avoided through systems thinking. If the potential impact of new students had been anticipated, plans to address that impact could have been prepared.

Systems Archetype

Remember that an archetype is simply a visual image of interactive events. This visual image is created through the use of balancing and reinforcing feedback systems.

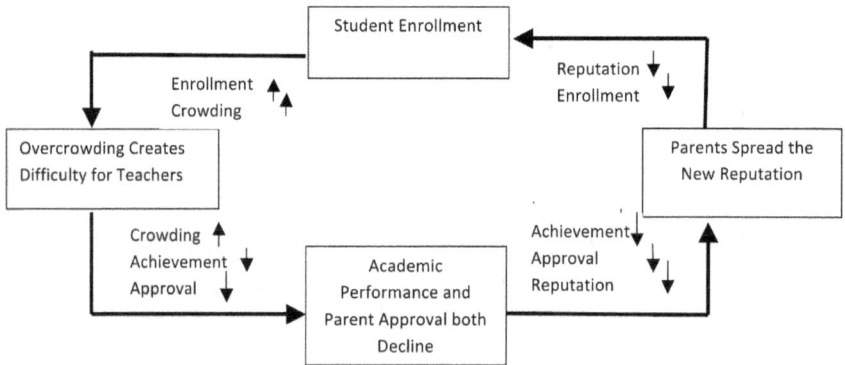

Figure 5.7.

It should be noted that numerous archetypes have been identified. In the Mental Models and Team Learning sections of this chapter, a diagram (actually an archetype) was used to assist in explaining the discipline. That archetype is called an escalation archetype because each action taken by one participant drives the other participant to engage in an action that "ups the ante" and thus escalates the situation. The danger of engaging in a pattern of antagonistic events is that once the escalation archetype is fully activated, it becomes a pure win/lose situation. The only way to avoid this is to recognize the pattern soon enough to find a compromise and shut off its progression. This is a very common archetype that is found in both interpersonal situations and in activities between and among organizations.

A second common archetype is called shifting the burden. The name is derived from the fact that we often respond to a problem by taking the easy way out. This may provide a short-term solution, but the ultimate result is that the problem is simply shifted to another part of the system. This is demonstrated in the following scenario and depicted in the archetype on the following page.

Consider the case of a school district faced with declining enrollment due to competition from several charter schools that have opened. The decline in enrollment causes a reduction in funding and creates pressure on the existing budget. In order to meet the new budget constraints, a decision is made to lay off personnel in the curriculum and professional development departments (a symptomatic or short-term solution). The reduction in salaries does relieve some of the pressure on the budget, but it also lowers the quality of service to teachers and ultimately to the program being offered to students. The lower-quality academic program leads to a further decline in the enrollment and additional loss of funding. This increases the pressure on the budget. A better (long-term) response would have been to increase the effectiveness of the curriculum and professional development departments and, as a result, offer a higher-quality program that would retain current students and attract new students.

It is difficult to just think through all the ramifications of a reduction in personnel. The use of a shifting the burden archetype creates a visual representation that is easier to grasp.

Pressure on the budget is the presenting symptom of the issue. Loop 1 depicts how when the pressure on the budget goes up, so does the need for a reduction in personnel. When the reductions take place, the pressure on the budget goes down. This is the short-term solution. Remember—the easy way out usually leads back in!

When loop 1 is activated, it sets in motion a series of unintended consequences that are seen in loop 3. The reduction in curriculum and professional development personnel results in a reduction of services to

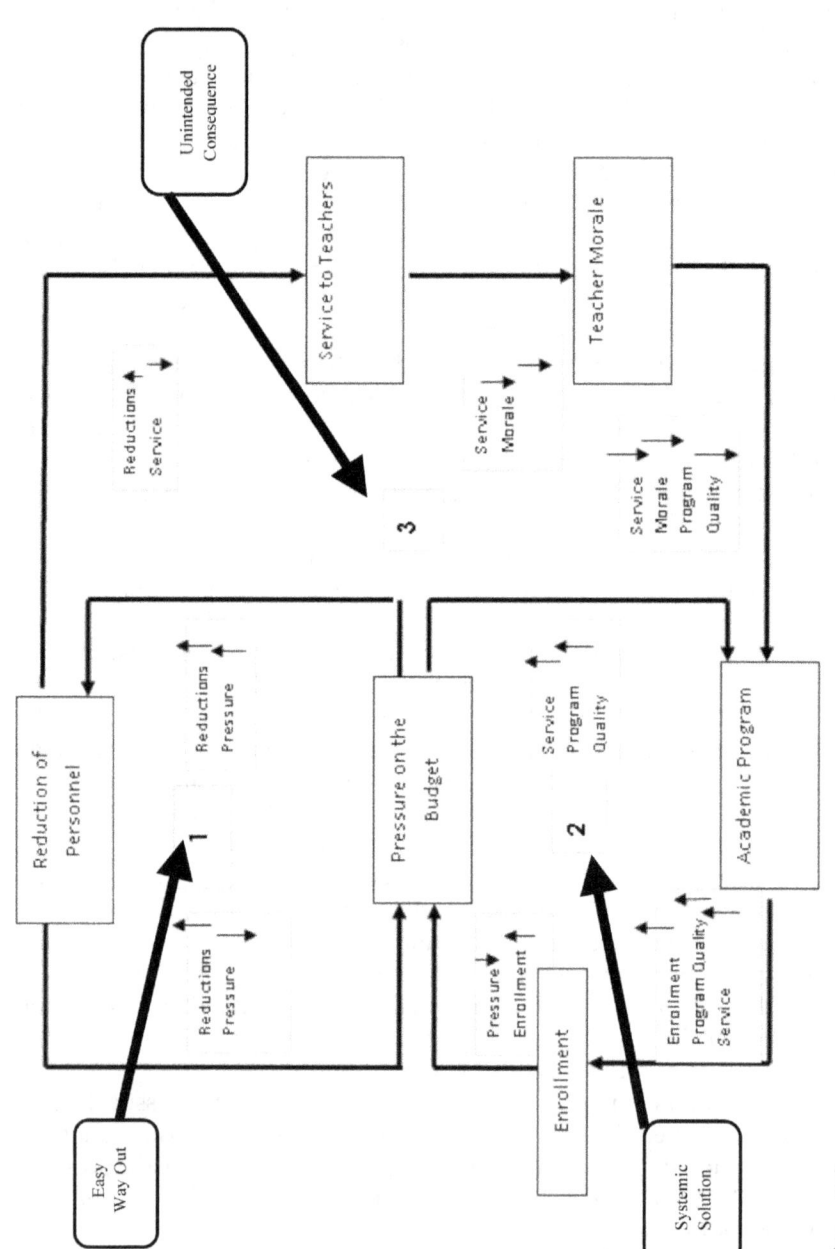

Figure 5.8.

teachers. The reduction in services is frustrating to teachers and results in a decline in morale. The low morale negatively impacts the quality of programs offered to students.

A better approach would have been to put in place the long-term solution that is depicted in loop 2. By elevating the services provided to teachers, the quality of the program could be enhanced. When the quality of the program is enhanced, new students could be attracted and prior students recovered. The increased enrollment would bring in additional funds and relieve the pressure on the budget. Activating loop 3 has a negative impact on the academic program and makes the successful activation of loop 2 much more difficult due to the loss of service and decline in morale.

Systems archetypes can be very powerful tools, and I encourage you to read the many books available on the topic.

SARGE'S STORY

The last month had been devoted to learning about the work of Dr. Senge. Each member of the leadership team was given a copy of *The Fifth Discipline*. A book study was arranged with teams of two each being assigned to one of the first four disciplines. Sarge was assigned to systems thinking. The task for each of the two-member teams was to teach the remainder of the leadership team about the discipline to which they had been assigned. The leadership team met several times to accomplish this task and the dialogue was very beneficial.

> Dr. S.: Alan, give me your assessment concerning what has occurred during the book study with the leadership team.
>
> Sarge: I think this has been a very valuable experience. The leadership team is functioning more effectively now that they understand team learning and the role of dialogue. What I learned about systems thinking has already had an impact and I'm sure it will have a greater impact in the future as I continue to learn about it.
>
> Dr. S.: Tell me how you see this has influenced the leadership team.
>
> Sarge: They seldom argue anymore. Jim has really made us abide by the rules of dialogue. They don't ridicule each other's ideas like they used to do. When we are dealing with a problem, we actually list possible solutions on the board and explore them without someone defending the one they suggested. One time, we actually used that shifting the burden archetype you taught us to anticipate the unintended consequences!
>
> Dr. S.: Congratulations, that is very encouraging to hear. How would you describe your current relationship with the leadership team as opposed to when we first formed the team?

Sarge: It is very different now. I now know that they are very dedicated to doing the right thing for the kids and I trust them to do just that. Now, the team openly puts forth their thoughts. They don't just sit there waiting for me to give orders. When we are having a dialogue, I usually only enter in when I know there is some law, rule, or district requirement that is being violated or to ask what they want me to do to communicate and support the action we have decided to take.

Dr. S.: Did you personally take anything specific away from the chapter you reviewed on systems thinking?

Sarge: Yes. Earlier this week, the school district curriculum director came to inform me of a new pacing guide that has been developed and that he expected me to ensure that teachers followed it. He was a bit taken aback when I asked about how teachers would be introduced to the guide and trained to use it. I also asked how this was to be used with the district-required lesson plans. I told him that I expected a great deal of resistance from the teachers as they would feel the need to push the kids too fast. He agreed but had no answer as to how to address the concerns that I had raised. As he left my office, he told me that I had raised questions that his department had not considered. I had to resist giving him a lesson on systems thinking.

Dr. S.: I think that was a good choice, but consider offering to meet with his department to engage in a dialogue concerning the implementation of the new guide.

Sarge: OK, I will do that but I want to meet with our leadership team first. I'm sure that they will give me a solid teacher perspective and I will be smarter when I meet with the district folks.

Dr. S.: We have been engaged in this adventure for almost an entire school year and I can see a change in you and how the school is functioning. Tell me how you see things.

Sarge: I think that I have changed a great deal. I now trust the teachers to do what is right for the kids and don't feel like I have to order them to do things anymore. The school is a very different place. The teachers really do work together. The real-time data that we collect is a topic in every meeting we hold. The level of student achievement has gone up steadily from the start of the year and we all feel good about how the kids will do on the state test. We still have some work to do to live up to the core commitments. We do talk about them and I expect them to be a major topic as we plan for next year.

Dr. S.: I'm really proud of how you have responded to the very difficult issues that you faced at the beginning of the year. Let's work very closely with the leadership team to plan the end-of-year review meetings to ensure that the good things you have all done this year will carry over to next year and become even more refined.

Sarge: Yes, I would like to do that.

As I thought about introducing Senge's work to Sarge and the leadership team, I included how I saw the impact in my mind map. We were already working on the discipline of shared vision through ongoing dialogue concerning the academic mission and the core commitments. I felt that focusing the leadership team on the disciplines of team learning and systems thinking would have the most impact in moving forward with the Continuous Improvement System.

My mind map was now complete. A full explanation of the map will be given in the next chapter.

The final section of the mind map depicts how the leadership team learned to use systems thinking to impact the school's structure and

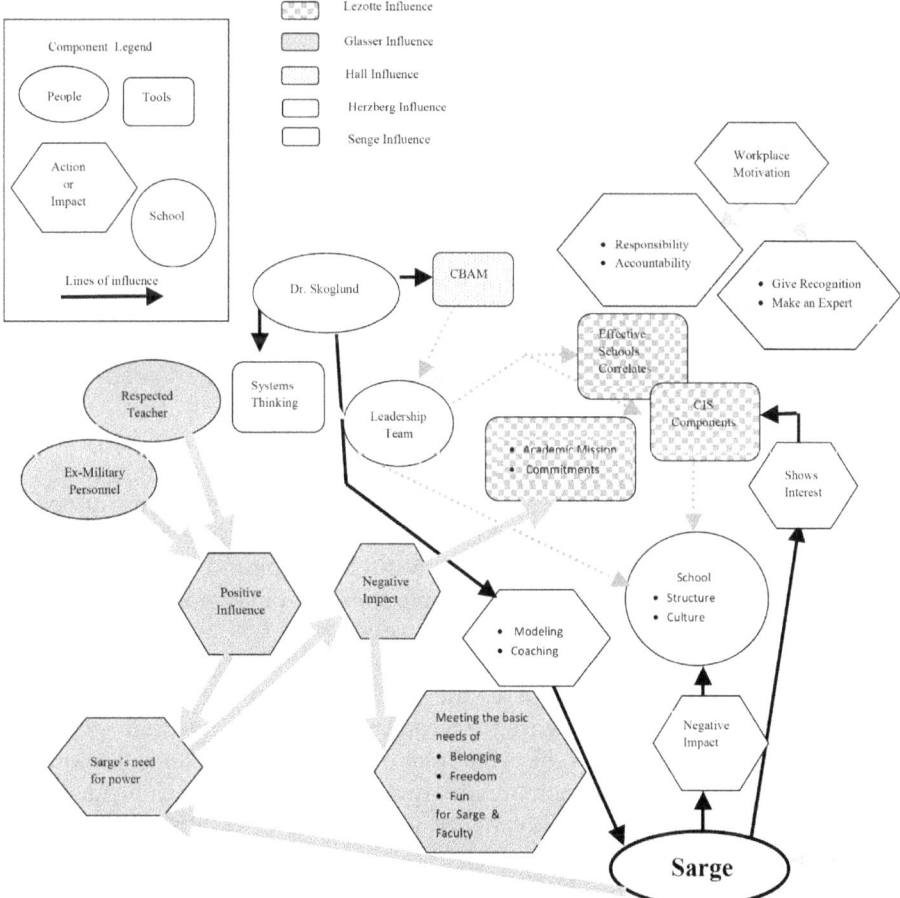

Figure 5.9.

culture through the implementation of the Continuous Improvement System.

SUMMARY

- *Webster's Dictionary* defines a system as a group of interrelated and interacting elements that form a complex whole.
- The world does not consist of disjointed parts. The world consists of an endless array of interacting systems.
- The organizations that will prosper in the future are the ones that will learn to see the patterns created by these interacting systems and then learn to adapt to the ever-changing environment.
- Organizations that learn will do so through the consistent pursuit of five disciplines:
  1. A shared vision drives an organization, not because the people have been forced to pursue the vision but because the people believe in the vision and willingly pursue it for its own value.
  2. Personal mastery is the never-ending pursuit of becoming the best we can be. It requires that the current reality is accurately identified and acknowledged. Then the focus must become acquiring the knowledge and skills required to attain a personal vision.
  3. Mental models are formed by the accumulation of our life's experiences and cause us to see the world as we do. We must learn to identify not only others' mental models but our own as well. Mental models can influence us to either engage in productive dialogue or lead us into escalating conflict.
  4. Team learning is the event that occurs when people genuinely collaborate to address an issue. Team learning has two components: The first is dialogue—the free flow of ideas that are examined and either enhanced or discarded. This is the time for exploration. After ideas have been thoroughly explored, the advocacy component is employed as people speak out in support of a given solution. This is the time to make decisions.
  5. Systems thinking fuses the first four disciplines into a coherent whole. It is the ability to see the individual components of a system and understand how they interact and how a change in one component will impact the remainder of the system. Systems thinking requires the collection and analysis of accurate data. Conclusions based on assumptions can lead to catastrophic results.

NOTHING STANDS ALONE!

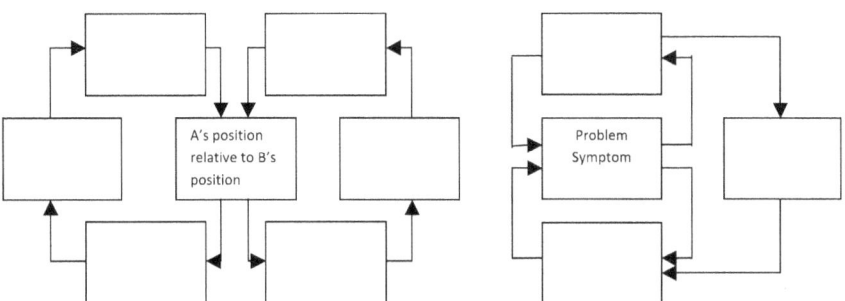

Figure 5.10. Escalation   Figure 5.11. Shifting the Burden

YOUR TASK

This time, you have some options: (1) choose either the escalation or the shifting the burden archetype and use it to analyze something that is currently happening in your organization or (2) identify something that is currently happening in your organization and create a mind map that helps you to identify all the aspects of the situation and what forces are influencing them.

_____
_____
_____
_____

6

The Mind Map

For me, the works of Hall, Herzberg, Glasser, Lezotte, and Senge will forever be inextricably interwoven. The mind map shown in figure 6.1 is an example of how this can occur.

Knowing that people resist change is of little value if you do not understand the basic human needs that underlie the resistance. You cannot assist people to work through their resistance unless you understand how to facilitate change. Identifying the need to elevate the effectiveness of an organization is easy but the question then becomes, how do you create an environment in which people will choose to perform at a high level while continuing to seeking new knowledge and skills? You have little chance of bringing effective change to an organization unless you understand the connections between and among the individual components of the organization.

Creating the mind map was extremely helpful in identifying the issues that were associated directly with Sarge and those that existed within the structure and culture of the school. It clearly depicts how the tools in the toolbox interact to form a system.

PHASE ONE: THE INFLUENCE OF DR. LEZOTTE

The first phase of the map was created as a response to my initial conversations with Sarge. It was intended to visually represent the negative impact that Sarge's decisions and resulting behavior were having on the

Photo 6.1.   Hall, Herzberg, Glasser, Lezotte, and Senge

school's operational structure and culture. It also depicts the interventions I planned to use.

Sarge brought a great deal of change to the school in the form of new policies, procedures, and communication processes. He, by virtue of his behavior, also represented a significant change. He was having a very difficult time shedding his military persona. His need to be in charge and his "here

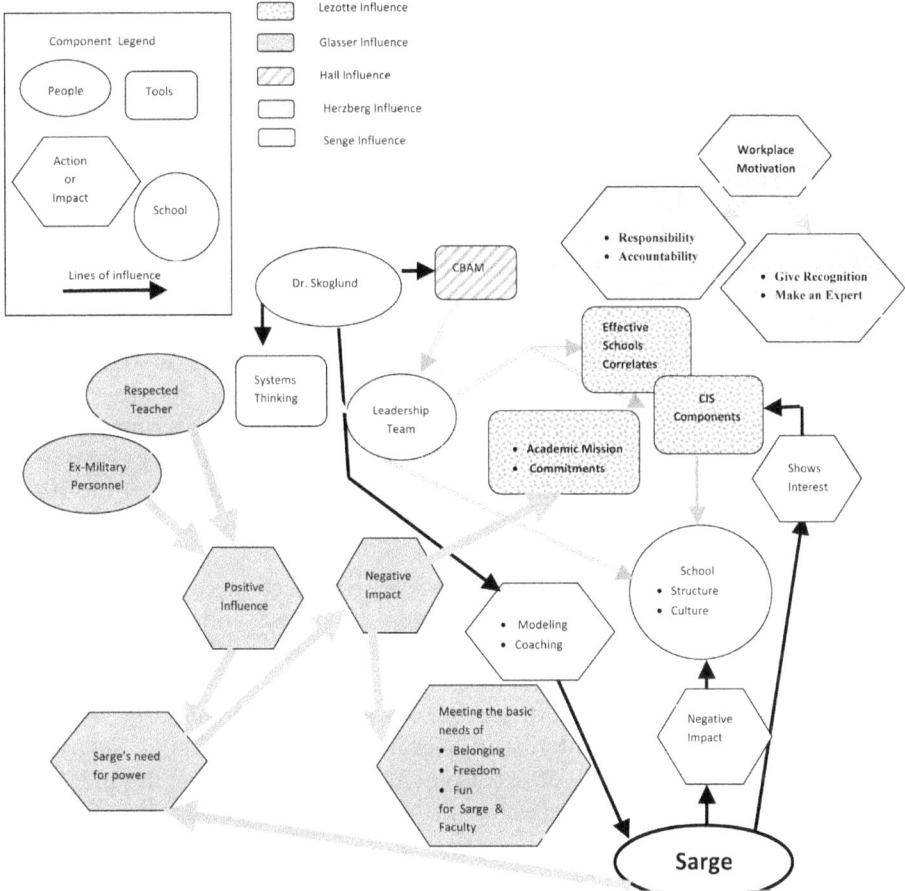

Figure 6.1.

are your marching orders" approach was having a profound impact on the culture of the school and on how the school operated on a daily basis.

As a result of my initial interviews with Sarge, it was obvious that he had little or no knowledge concerning the successful administration of an effective school. This made it critical to create a picture in his mind of what a successful school looks like. The Effective Schools Correlates clearly portray how the different aspects of an effective school should look and function. Following a thorough study of the concepts that underlie the correlates, Sarge needed an organizational structure that would enable him to take these concepts and convert them into hands-on practices that could be implemented in the school. The Continuous Improvement System provided this structure.

We studied the CIS in detail. It was gratifying to see that Sarge was able to identify how the Effective Schools Correlates formed the foundation of the CIS. Sarge admitted that he knew little of how to administer a school and thought that the structure of the CIS would be very helpful. He declared that he was interested in learning about the CIS and implementing it in the school as quickly as possible.

However, implementing the CIS takes time and patience. It cannot be done successfully by the principal just issuing an order. It requires everyone in the school to be involved. Sarge agreed to work closely with me (to actually allow me to direct him) as the CIS was introduced to the faculty. Initially, I personally conducted the orientation and training meetings. My intent was to give Sarge a role model to follow when he would have to conduct the meetings. Later, we planned the meetings together and then he would conduct the meetings. We debriefed after each meeting, and I coached him on better ways to deal with situations that came up in the meeting and how to respond to situations we were anticipating. As he became more comfortable with using new behaviors, he was able to analyze his own performance.

As he gained knowledge about how the CIS functioned, he agreed to tone down his typical "here are your orders" approach and engage teachers in a more collegial manner. This relieved much of the tension that existed between him and the faculty.

This plan did not solve all the problems that surrounded Sarge, but it did result in his honest interest in learning about the Effective Schools Correlates and the CIS. His effort also demonstrated to the faculty that he was working to become an effective principal. This was a very important step in the right direction.

PHASE TWO: THE INFLUENCE OF DR. GLASSER

We had considered the needs of the school itself and now it was time to consider Sarge's personal needs. The work of Dr. William Glasser was used to begin to address this very volatile situation.

A lengthy and rather intense conversation led me to believe that Sarge's experience at the school was in no way meeting any of his basic psychological needs. Most significantly, Sarge exhibited an overwhelming need for power. He needed to be in control and ensure that people knew he was the one in control. This was alienating the faculty and preventing him from experiencing success in the basic psychological needs of belonging, freedom, and fun. His own behavior was costing him dearly. His frustration with his personal situation was surfacing as confrontational behavior that was having a very negative impact on the needs of the general faculty. This created a culture that was very guarded and made collaboration with and among the teachers virtually impossible.

To teach Sarge about the basic psychological needs, I began by using the feelings he experienced when the superintendent demanded that he check in on everything he wanted to do. We then explored how his need for power was negatively impacting the basic psychological needs of the faculty. His need for power was very evident when the faculty met to write the academic mission and he dominated the meeting.

Adjusting to civilian life was very difficult for Sarge, and assisting him in this area seemed to be the logical starting point to help him to change his behavior. Lecturing him on how to act would not have been well received and might possibly have entrenched him deeper in his current confrontational behavior. I chose instead to place Sarge in situations where his psychological needs could be met. A three-pronged approach that included my influence, the influence of a trusted teacher, and the influence of ex-military personnel to whom he could relate appeared to offer the best opportunity to influence the behaviors that were driven by his need for power.

He needed a soft sell from people he trusted. We were fortunate to have available recently retired military personnel who were willing to befriend Sarge and help him through the transition from military to civilian life. The personal relationships that developed gave Sarge a group that began to meet his need to belong. His new friends were able to guide him and even, in good fun, tease him into examining some of his mental models and adopting new behaviors. At that time, none of these men had any idea of what a mental model was, but identifying and examining them was exactly what they were doing.

Hearing the perspective of a teacher whom he trusted helped Sarge to see his own behavior through the eyes of the people he was assigned to lead. It was through dialogue with this teacher that he was able to understand how his controlling behavior had interfered with the faculty writing and buying into the academic mission. The faculty did see him as a leader but not in any way the type of leader described in the Effective Schools Correlates.

PHASE THREE: THE INFLUENCE OF DR. HALL

Sarge's background had entrenched a mental model that the way to get things done was to issue orders. This approach was clearly not working with the faculty. He needed a better understanding of how long-term change occurs and the skills to facilitate such change. Dr. Gene Hall's Concerns-Based Adoption Model (CBAM) provided what was needed.

The leadership team and Sarge needed to enhance their ability to work together and be seen as a unified group leading the school. Studying the CBAM was an important step in bringing them together. Following a detailed explanation, they spent time practicing by interviewing each other and identifying the stages of concern they heard. Each member of the team was then assigned to engage two faculty members in a dialogue that began with the question, "When you think about implementing the Continuous Improvement System in our school, what is your greatest concern?" The team was able to sort the concerns they heard into three groups—information concerns, personal concerns, and management concerns. Using this information, the team carefully designed very specific interventions to address each of the concerns. The team presented these interventions in a faculty meeting and followed up with individual teachers.

This was a solid step in the right direction. The faculty was now beginning to feel that they were being heard, and they became more willing to discuss their concerns. As time passed, the faculty realized that their concerns were being addressed and the resistance to changes that were being made decreased dramatically.

The use of the CBAM by the leadership team advanced the implementation of the CIS and had a very positive impact on the culture of the school.

PHASE FOUR: THE INFLUENCE OF DR. HERZBERG

Sarge was developing a better working relationship with the faculty. He had learned to become a contributing member of the leadership team and was no longer an overpowering influence. He was learning to listen to the concerns that were being voiced and to respond appropriately to those concerns. The leadership team had developed a very collegial relationship. Now was an ideal time to employ Dr. Herzberg's motivation in the workplace techniques to keep them moving and growing.

I decided to use the job satisfaction factor of recognition and the vertical job loading principle of becoming an expert with Sarge. I frequently provided positive feedback in private and recognized him for his work in front of the faculty at every opportunity. Sarge and I discussed at least one aspect of the CIS every time we were together. He had gained a solid working knowledge of the individual components and was now perceived by the faculty as the resident expert on the CIS. He recognized his personal mastery reality concerning the CIS and frequently contacted me to discuss issues that had surfaced. This was important as he was sincerely seeking growth. The fact that the faculty now held this perception was what was important. This perception had a very positive impact on his need to belong and reinforced his growing ability to appropriately use power.

Sarge and I decided to use two vertical job loading principles with the leadership team. We asked the leadership team to accept more responsibility for ensuring the effective functioning of the instructional teams. We met often to discuss the performance of the teams. These discussions created a real sense of accountability for the individual members of the leadership team.

PHASE FIVE: THE INFLUENCE OF DR. SENGE

Due to our work with the Effective Schools Correlates and our detailed study of *The Fifth Discipline*, Sarge and the leadership team were beginning to understand how the school functioned as a complex system. The leadership team was eager to have the faculty repeat their experience. They wanted to immediately engage the faculty in a book study of each of the disciplines. We analyzed this plan by giving consideration to the Concerns-Based Adoption Model. The team quickly realized that this would be too much—too fast. The team then developed a plan to introduce two of the disciplines. Introducing a shared vision was a natural choice because of the work that was already being done on the academic mission and the core commitments. Each of the leadership team members was assigned to a grade level and began to attend their regular meetings. Items concerning the academic mission and the core commitments were added to the standing agendas. As the dialogue progressed, more and more teachers expressed their support for the mission and the commitments. People were now pursuing the mission and the commitments, not because they were told to but because they felt these documents accurately and fairly portrayed what needed to happen in the school.

The second discipline to be introduced was systems thinking. Sarge explained this discipline in a faculty meeting by relating the story of his conversation with the curriculum director concerning the new pacing guide. The faculty was then divided into small groups and engaged in a gamelike activity. Each group was given a topic related to some activity in the school. They were challenged to find all the other aspects of the school that would be affected if this activity was to change in some way. They were free to determine what change would take place. There was a great deal of talk and laughter during the exercise, but people really seemed to grasp the idea of the school as a collection of interactive components that formed a system. The concept of systems thinking quickly became a frequent topic of conversation as new ideas and practices were introduced in the school. As the interest in systems thinking grew, the leadership team distributed four- to five-page documents that gave overviews of the other three disciplines. These were discussed in faculty meetings during the remainder of the year. The leadership team began to make plans for the next school year. A professional development program that would encourage personal mastery became the highest priority.

SARGE'S STORY

There was still much work to be done, but at the end of the year both Sarge and the school were functioning more effectively. The change in Sarge was remarkable. He had let go of most of his controlling behaviors. This change had allowed him to develop a much healthier relationship with the faculty. Now people stayed and talked with him when he entered the teachers' lounge instead of making hasty exists when he entered. The superintendent had stopped looking over his shoulder at every move. He often brought back a funny story about his weekend golf game. All four of his basic psychological needs were now being met to some degree.

The pursuit of personal mastery that made him so successful in the military was again evident. Now, however, he was working hard to develop his knowledge of how schools function and what makes them effective. He often requested feedback from me and from the teacher whom he trusted. He wanted to understand how his leadership behavior was impacting the school. Even though he had been a marine, he was focused on the army slogan—"Be all that you can be."

During the end-of-year faculty meeting, the faculty put on a skit in which they had Sarge come to the front of the room dressed in a shirt that had sergeant stripes attached to the sleeves. Two teachers came forward and presented him with a new dress shirt. The shirt had the school mascot on the pocket. He was also given a tie in the school colors. They assisted him to put this on over the "Sarge" shirt. A third teacher then presented Sarge with a nameplate for his desk that read: "Mr. Alan Wilson, Principal."

Not all stories of schools and/or principals in trouble have happy endings. If the individual(s) charged with changing the school and/or principal skillfully use the tools that have been introduced in this book, the opportunity for a successful change is greatly enhanced. Learning to apply these tools has fascinated me throughout my professional career. I am still learning and strongly encourage you to assemble your own toolbox. You will enjoy selecting the tools and greatly benefit from learning to use them effectively.

SUMMARY

- Principals and faculty leaders are the primary change agents in a school. These people must remember well Dr. Hall's words, "Organizations will not change until the people change."
- When you are attempting to bring about change in a large organization, focus on the people first and then the innovation.
- The ability to plan and anticipate the ramifications of implementing a plan is critical to successful change.
- Change takes time. "Change is a process, not an event."—Dr. Gene Hall
- Never stop the pursuit of personal mastery.

YOUR TASK

This is, perhaps, the most important task you have been asked to accomplish. It is intended to make you think of the toolbox as a system.

Analyze what you believe may have happened if:

- Only Lezotte's Effective Schools Correlates and the components of the Continuous Improvement System were introduced in the school.
- Only Glasser's basic psychological needs were taught to the faculty and the faculty was then asked to take care of each other.
- Only Hall's Concerns-Based Adoption Model had been taught to Mr. Wilson and the leadership team.
- Only Herzberg's job satisfaction factors had been taught to Mr. Wilson and the leadership team.
- Senge's concept of the school as a system had been taught to only Mr. Wilson and the leadership team.
- The tools were applied individually and not collectively.

_____
_____
_____
_____

7

The Perfect Storm

The demand for productivity and accountability from our schools is, perhaps, greater today than at any other time in our nation's history. This is occurring in the face of what Dr. Lezotte describes as the *perfect storm.* In 2009, Dr. Lezotte received the prestigious Brock International Prize in Education. In his acceptance speech, he presented a paper in which he discussed the coming together of several *trends that are creating the perfect storm* in the educational community. These trends are listed below:

- *The need to remain competitive in the world markets has led business, industry, and political leaders to demand higher educational standards and more demanding assessments.* Simply raising the standards does not mean that students are prepared to jump to new heights. The fact that student achievement scores have not soared is being looked upon by many as the failure of the American school system. This has resulted in a loss of confidence in schools and the search for alternative educational paths.
- *The demographic profile of the United States is changing rapidly and dramatically.* For a myriad of reasons, many students are entering school, at all grade levels, poorly prepared to succeed. Among these reasons are poor academic preparation, language and/or cultural barriers, and a background of indifference to education. These are societal issues that far exceed the school's ability to solve. We learned from Dr. Senge that the shifting the burden archetype would suggest that a systemic (societal) approach is necessary to adequately address these

issues. That has not occurred, and schools are left to struggle with the symptomatic issues that become so very evident in the classrooms.
- *Educational resources are being reduced at an alarming rate.* Politicians at both the federal and state levels have turned to making severe cuts in education funding in an attempt to address budget deficits. This has led to issues such as the inability to attract talented people into the educational profession due to low salaries, the need for teachers to purchase classroom supplies out of pocket, the decline of facilities, and an overall decline in morale. It is ironic that the same politicians whose actions have exacerbated the problems are now calling the educational system a failure. If we are to believe the political rhetoric that a highly educated and youthful workforce is the key to our future, then we must hold our political leaders accountable for acting in a manner that is true to their words.

I am firmly convinced that the primary determinant of the quality of education that a student experiences is the quality of instruction the student receives on a daily basis. If we proceed from that premise, it is obvious that we must focus on producing the most capable educators possible. With consideration to the aforementioned trends, what must be done to accomplish this?

First and foremost, the education profession must be elevated to a level that will make it possible to attract and retain the best and brightest. This will require our political leaders to recognize that salaries and working conditions in education must be comparable to what the best and brightest can expect to experience in other professions. Elevating the status of the profession will also require a change of image. This will involve the media's portrayal of the profession, the manner in which political leaders and the leaders of business and industry speak of the profession, and how we, as educators, speak of the profession. Finally, people entering education must be prepared to perform as professionals on the job and conduct themselves as professionals in the community.

As a district-level administrator, I frequently hired teachers and building administrators. It was my experience that teachers came to the classroom with considerable content knowledge but often lacked the teaching skills necessary to successfully impart that knowledge to their students. Administrators came with procedural knowledge (they could create a budget) but often lacked the skills to cause the people around them to perform at the highest level. These things are glaring shortcomings of the university training programs. The lack of these critical skills can be partially addressed through district-level professional development programs, but this should not be necessary.

The Perfect Storm

It is unrealistic to ask teachers to work harder. The load they carry is already crushing. Therefore, any technology application that can lighten the load for teachers should be explored. Technology can play an important role in planning, record keeping, data production, and analysis. There are also some excellent programs that can be purchased or accessed online that can be effectively used by a teacher to work with students.

Technology, however, must not be seen as a replacement for a teacher!

The true teaching/learning process requires an interpersonal connection that can never be replaced by a computer. I have yet to witness a former student return to his or her school, run up to a computer, embrace it, and say, "Thank you for all that you did for me."

> The improvement of our schools is directly linked to the performance of the educators working in the schools. It is time for educators and political leaders to come together and commit to building a shared vision of highly qualified educators leading students to higher levels of achievement. The Continuous Improvement System and the tools described in this book can play significant roles in accomplishing such a shared vision!

References

Bohm, David. 1996. *On Dialogue*. New York: Routledge.

Chadderdon, Lisa. 1999. "In the VC Derby, Jockeys Come Up Short." Retrieved from www.fastcompany.com/37451/vc-derby-jockeys-come-short.

Coleman, James. 1966. *Equality of Educational Opportunity Study*. Washington: U.S. Office of Education.

Glasser, William. 1984. *Control Theory: A New Explanation of How We Control Our Lives*. New York: Harper & Row.

Hall, Gene, and Shirley Hord. 2006. *Implementing Change: Patterns, Principles, and Potholes*. Boston: Pearson Education.

Herzberg, Frederick. 1993. *The Motivation to Work*. London: Transaction Publishers.

Kohn, Alfie. 1993. *Punished by Rewards*. New York: Houghton Mifflin.

Lezotte, Lawrence. 2009. "Effective Schools: Past, Present, and Future." Presented at the Brock Symposium on Excellence in Education. Effective Schools Products, Okemos, MI.

Lortie, Dan. 1975. *Schoolteacher: A Sociological Study*. London: University of Chicago Press.

Senge, Peter. 1990. *The Fifth Discipline*. New York: Bantam Doubleday Dell.

———. 2000. *Schools That Learn*. New York: Doubleday Dell.

Skoglund, Frederic, and Judy Ness. 2011. *Student Success: How to Make It Happen*. Lanham, MD: Rowman & Littlefield.

Suggested Reading

Glasser, William. 1986. *Control Theory in the Classroom.* New York: Harper & Row.
———. 1998. *Choice Theory: A New Psychology of Personal Freedom.* New York: Harper Collins.
Hord, Shirley, and Gene Hall. 1989. *Taking Charge of Change.* Austin, TX: Southwest Educational Development Laboratory.
Lezotte, Lawrence. 1997. *Learning for All.* Okemos, MI: Effective Schools Products.
———. 2002. *Assembly Required.* Okemos, MI: Effective Schools Products.
Lezotte, Lawrence, and Kathleen McKee Snyder. 2011. *What Effective Schools Do.* Okemos, MI: Effective Schools Products.
Lezotte, Lawrence, and Jo-Ann Pepperl. 1999. *The Effective Schools Process: A Proven Path to Learning for All.* Okemos, MI: Effective Schools Products.
———. 2006. [A series] *What Effective Schools Research Says: Clear and Focused Mission/ Opportunity to Learn, Frequent Monitoring of Student Achievement, High Expectations, Safe and Orderly Environment, Positive Home–School Relations.* Okemos, MI: Effective Schools Products.
O'Connor, Joseph, and Ian McDermott. 1997. *The Art of Systems Thinking.* San Francisco: HarperCollins.
Oshry, Barry. 1996. *Seeing Systems: Unlocking the Mysteries of Organizational Life.* San Francisco: Berrett-Koehler.
Popham, W. James. 1995. *Classroom Assessment: What Teachers Need to Know.* Needham Heights, MA: Allyn & Bacon.
Senge, Peter. 1994. *The Fifth Discipline Fieldbook.* New York: Doubleday.
Skoglund, Frederic. 1999. "How to Address Inadequacy of Classroom Performance." *Journal of Personnel Evaluation in Education* 13 (3): 297–306.

About the Author

Following a distinguished career in public school administration, capped by fifteen years of service as the assistant superintendent for secondary education in Arizona's largest school district, Dr. Frederic W. Skoglund founded the Viking Solutions educational consulting organization.

Dr. Skoglund's primary focus is working directly in underperforming schools. He has been highly successful in assisting administrators and teachers in many schools to raise the level of student achievement. He also works at the district level developing teacher evaluation instruments and intervention programs. He is the lead author of *Student Success: How to Make It Happen*.

Dr. Skoglund lives in Mesa, Arizona, and can be reached at fskoglund@aol.com. You may learn more about his work by visiting www.vikingsolutions.net.

www.ingramcontent.com/pod-product-compliance
Lightning Source LLC
Chambersburg PA
CBHW052134300426
44116CB00010B/1892